MARRIAGE CEREMONIES

The affectionate Adieu of Hector and Andromache.

Published by J. Bumpus, 6 Holborn

MARRIAGE CUSTOMS

MARRIAGE CUSTOMS

AND

Modes of Courtship

OF THE

VARIOUS NATIONS

BY

THEOPHILUS MOORE, ESQ.

But happy they, the happiest of their kind,
Who in each other clasp whatever fair
High fancy forms, or lavish hearts can wish.
THOMSON.

SECOND EDITION

GYAN

Published by

Gyan Publishing House
5, Ansari Road
Daryaganj, New Delhi-110002
Phone: 011-47034999, 9811692060
E-mail: books@gyanbooks.com

Distribution Network
gyanbooks.com
India, USA, Canada, UK, Australia, France

ISBN : 978-81-212-6097-8 (PB)
First Published, 1820

2nd Impression 2021

Printed at: Gyan Press, Delhi.

Marriage Customs and Modes of Courtship of the Various Nations
Author: Theophilus Moore

MARRIAGE CUSTOMS

AND

Modes of Courtship

OF THE

VARIOUS NATIONS

By THEOPHILUS MOORE, Esq.

But happy they, the happiest of their kind,
Who in each other clasp whatever fair
High fancy forms, or lavish hearts can wish.—

THOMSON.

SECOND EDITION.

1820.

PREFACE.

PRODUCTIONS of the nature of this work can possess little other merit than that of accurate selection, and their utility or entertainment principally consists in presenting, under a brief view, information dispersed throughout a number of expensive and elaborate volumes, in which references are occasionally made to the subjects mentioned in our title. It is interesting and important to the observing mind to compare the different sentiments which every where respect the relative situations of man and wife, to observe the customs with which different nations cement the conjugal union, and the condition of the sex in society. It should seem in proportion as women are admitted to their natural rights and weight in the scale of existence, the character of the man is softened, and states are recognized by a love of the arts and sciences; since a relish for cultivating the society of women presupposes a tendency to civilization and harmony. The purpose of this little volume is fully answered if it create a sigh in the bosom of our fair countrywomen for the afflicting situation in which rude laws and savage customs have placed the young and amiable part of their sex, and raise a feeling of gratitude to that Being who has cast their lot in a Christian country, and under British laws and opinions, which give equal protection to all, and require no sacrifices inconsistent with good order and common sense.

In these pages, the object has been not to influence the passions, but to temper and model them to prudence and virtue. Pleasure, it is justly observed, is a most seducing thing; it is the idol which all the world worship; therefore it behoves the young to guard cautiously against being carried away in its stream, and ingulphed in its consequences. It tempts youth in a thousand different shapes; and when the mind is early given to the delicious *delusion*, and that again is strengthened by habit and thoughtless society, it will be hard, if not impossible, to recover any one in such a state to relish that which is rational, serious, and of the greatest concern. When the employment of life is wound up, and youth has insensibly sunk into decrepitude and decay, what comfort can arise from the recollection of days, nights, and years, consumed in the perpetual succession of toilsome and unprofitable amusements! Higher views and employments become every one. All may virtuously sip at the fountain of pleasure, not plunge in, and thus augment physical gratification by giving a preponderancy to the dictates of that more noble part which never dies.

PREFACE.

Among the various societies formed for relieving the wants of the human race, no one has yet arisen for ameliorating the condition of women, in countries where their situation is intolerable. The medium of the prince is perhaps the only one; but where shall we find one sufficiently liberal to be consulted on such a delicate subject? Jealousy or power interfere, and it is, perhaps, the last effort that will be made to humanize the rude and unfeeling dominion which strength gives man over woman. Could we but make men just, duty, as well as passion, would influence them to consider their wives as themselves, and to share equally with them the burthen and heat of the day. The accomplishment of this is devoutly to be wished, for the interest of religion and the dignity of human kind.

Calina Cottage, Surry. THE EDITOR.

CONTENTS.

AMATORY CUSTOMS,

&c. &c.

EUROPE.

IN no country is gallantry carried to such an extent as in France. A Frenchman piques himself upon being polished above the natives of any other country by his conversation with the fair sex. In the course of his communication (with which he is indulged from his most tender years,) he learns, like a parrot, by rote, the whole circle of French compliments, which are a set of phrases ridiculous even to a proverb; and those he throws out indiscriminately to all women without any distinction, in the exercise of that kind of address which is here distinguished by the name of gallantry. It is an exercise, by the repetition of which he becomes very pert, very familiar, and very impertinent. A Frenchman, in consequence of his mingling with the females from his infancy, not only becomes acquainted with all their customs and humours, but grows wonderfully alert in performing a thousand little offices which are overlooked by others whose time is more valuably occupied in making useful acquisitions. He enters, without ceremony, a lady's bed-chamber while she is in bed, reaches her whatever she may want, airs her chemise, and helps to put it on. He attends at her toilet, regulates the distribution of her patches, and advises her where to lay on the paint. If he visits when she is dressed, and perceives the least impropriety in her dress, he insists upon adjusting it with his own hands. If he sees her hair or a curl amiss, he produces his comb, scissars, and pomatum, and sets it to rights, with the dexterity of a professed friseur. He squires her to every place she visits, either on business or pleasure, and by thus dedicating his time to her, renders himself necessary to her occasions.

Mr. Williams, in his travels through France in 1812, remarks on the frivolity of these customs, and expresses his opinion of them in the following terms:—

"In no nation on earth do the married women

enjoy more liberty than in France; as they generally have their own plans of amusement, while the husband finds his out of the bosom of his family; we, therefore, rarely find that domestic comfort so frequently met with in our own country. A circumstance which appears singular to an Englishman, is that of a husband never giving his arm to his wife when they walk out; and if I may judge of others by myself, says Mr. W. we feel ourselves very awkward in putting on a lady's glove, or assisting her at the toilet. These, however, are all necessary accomplishments to those who wish to be well received by *madame;* and as I never wish to be the last in attentions to the fairer part of the creation, I have, with some difficulty, become quite a proficient in the art; though I always put up a silent prayer that none of my English friends may catch me in the frivolous occupation."

The very festivals of fools in the middle ages were not more absurd than the courts of love, and the orders of love; the latter of which numbered many martyrs of their unexampled folly, but not of genuine affection. The proofs of gallantry exhibited by many knights of the Burgundian Court, of the sixteenth century, were perfectly consonant with the spirit of the more ancient courts and orders of love.

In the year 1468, at the magnificent tournament held by the Bastard of Burgundy, in honour of the Princess Margaret of England, the second wife of Charles the Bold, a Burgundian knight, Johan de Chasse, applied by the following letter, addressed to the ladies assembled on that occasion, for permission to be present at the exercises of chivalry.

"High and mighty Prince and Lady, and you, my other gracious Princesses and Ladies, permit a knight-slave, born in the kingdom of servitude, to announce to you his arrival in this noble city; and that, in the company of a lady-errant, to whose guidance he has been committed by his mistress. The knight-slave can, with truth assert, that he has, during his whole life, been held in servitude by a lady, and that, though she gave encouragement to his hopes, yet she never could resolve to accept him for her servant.

"As his love-sickness increased to such a degree that he was no longer able to endure its torments, he ventured, in a state of despairing hope, to implore mercy, favour, and an alleviation of his pain, of which he knew himself to be unworthy, but which he conceived he had deserved by his true and constant devotion. Notwithstanding this humble reqnest, the said lady still continuing in her haughty indifference, her disobedience to love, and her neglect of that female virtue, compassion, deprived him of all hope of ever enjoying happiness in this world; so that he retired, full of indignation and anguish, to a solitary habitation among rocks, mountains, and trackless forests, and there lived nine months on nothing but sorrow, sighs, and tears. Had this state lasted a little longer, the afflicted knight would soon have closed his earthly career. But, when the lady received intelligence of his condition, she was touched with remorse for culpable ingratitude, and sent the said lady-errant to represent to him that the raptures of love must be purchased by patience, long-suffering, and manifold tribulations; that the higher is the price paid for its pleasures, so much the more is its enjoyments; and that in love there is not a greater crime than despair. The lady therefore exhorted the knight-errant to indulge hope instead of despair, and to take courage instead of yielding to pusillanimity. The lady-errant likewise persuaded him to undertake a journey, in order to dissipate his grief. The fair one promising to accompany him a whole year for the purpose of consoling him in his affliction, and giving his mistress an account of his adventures. The knight followed this council, though he is from Sclavonia, and had no acquaintance in these regions. But as the said knight recollected that even divers infidels, especially the valiant Saladin, had come to France to acquire glory, and that they had experienced the most noble reception in this most noble kingdom; but induced more particularly by the fame and the sublime virtues of the exalted house of Burgundy, and the report that foreigners were no where better received, and that the exercises and feats of chivalry were no where more studiously cultivated than by that sublime house, he repaired hither, attended by the lady-errant, and met with his first fortunate adventure in the noble enterprize of the Knight of the Golden Tree, and the commencement of this tournament. He therefore intreats the sublime princess and lady, the Duchess of Burgundy, and the other princesses and ladies, to use their interest with the high and mighty Lord and Duke of Burgundy, to procure permission for him to take part in this same tournament, &c."

To this same tournament came a dwarf, riding upon a little white poney, having a petition in his left hand, and suspended from his right arm a key to a mysterious castle, which slowly advanced behind him. When the dwarf and the castle, which contained a Count de Roussy, on horseback, and in complete armour, arrived in front of the ladies' scaffold, he handed to them a petition to the following effect:—

"Sublime, illustrious, and noble princesses and ladies, the knight, who is held a prisoner by his lady, most respectfully salutes you. His situation is briefly this. Danger has possessed the key of this prison, and has placed it in the hands of Little Hope. The knight will never be able to procure his repose from this dungeon, unless through your favour and compassion. The captive knight therefore implores you, serene princesses and noble ladies, that you would assemble your virtuous council (for among many there might be one, to whom Danger would not refuse the deliverance of the knight) to the end that Little Hope, who conducts him, may be commanded to release the prisoner from his confinement, for otherwise he cannot take part in the present tournament, and assist in finishing the adventure of the Golden Tree, which he desires no less ardently than to remain the faithful servant of the illustrious princesses, and all the other noble ladies."

The petition of the knight was taken into consideration, and the ladies soon ordered that the knight should be released. The dwarf opened the door, and out sprang the Count de Roussy, on a horse beautifully caparisoned and clad in complete armour. A third knight was conducted into the list by a beautiful young lady, who bore the appellation of the *Dame Blanche*. She was dressed in white satin, was seated on a horse, and delivered to the ladies a poetic petition, in which she informed them that the knight was her servant, and that she therefore requested permission for him to show his prowess at the tournament of the Knight of the Golden Tree, in order that he might thereby render himself more worthy of her love.

If the gallantry of the ancient knight was

not ludicrous idolatry, it must, however, be admitted to have been childish play.

Tournaments were always concluded with a sumptuous dinner; but the entertainment of the fair was very different to what we might suppose. They were not (according to the etiquette of that age) allowed to mingle in the society of men, the sexes being seated at different tables. The only opportunity the men had of conversing with the ladies, was in attending them to and from the place where the tournament was held, and to and from their apartments. But the ladies always rode either on horseback or in litters to the tournament; therefore, there was little opportunity for paying respects to them, or showing any personal gallantries.

Among the knights of antiquity, it was common for them to devote themselves to the service of a lady whom they knew only by name. Many would purchase stockings for their own use, which they requested their mistresses to wear for a few days, by way of consecration, before they took them into wear themselves.

Courts of Love were held formerly among the knights and ladies, composed of persons of both sexes, who decided all cases between lovers and their mistresses; determined all points of etiquette in gallantry; and many other things, which would at the present day appear absurd and ridiculous in the extreme; such as settling the terms to be made use of by lovers or knights-errant to their mistresses, and not unfrequently between husbands and wives, assuming to themselves the power of arbitration between married persons.

Mr. Kotzbue relates many anecdotes, to show the present state of feeling with respect to matrimony, which, while they amuse by relation of facts, show the comparative excellence of a well-regulated system. We shall pass over his description of the fantastical and ridiculous dresses worn by the *élégants*, or men of fashion, which, thank heaven, with all our excesses, we have not yet become degraded enough servilely to imitate, and proceed to some anecdotes more nearly connected with the dissolute manners which sometimes prevail in our own capital; we mean the production of matrimonial matches, by advertising in the newspapers.

These kinds of advertisements are much more frequent in Paris than London, from the simple circumstance that the people of that capital are doubtless farther advanced in vice. The following are specimens of the Parisian mode of advertising, to which we shall subjoin M. Kotzebue's remarks.

"A bachelor of forty, versed in literature, a cheerful companion, of pleasing manners, *good family*, and in tolerable easy circumstances, wishes to meet with a maiden lady or widow, without children, *from twenty-six to thirty-four* years of age, well-bred, intelligent, and without property, to be united, *(à s'unir,)* and to live happily together."

Does this *unity* signify to *marry?* I do not know. At any rate one cannot help observing what stress the French lay upon being of a good family.

"A man, thirty-eight years old, who is his own master, &c. &c. wishes to find a lady who has some property, and would be willing to join in company with him." The word marry is again eluded.

"A healthy widower, sixty years old, without children, possessing a yearly income of 1400 francs, and who has for these ten years inhabited neat apartments in the Thuilleries, seeks a lady of a *suitable age*, of agreeable temper, and some property, to whom he might make such proposals as would be acceptable; or he is willing to receive proposals from her. His sole aim is their mutual happiness."

This old Carydon, likewise, is carefully not to mention matrimony. He too, like the former, makes it a condition that the lady must not be poor. For the rest it is worthy of remark, that he boasts of his lodgings being near the Thuilleries, a circumstance particularly tempting to a French woman.

"A young widow, in every respect interesting, both with regard to character, personal accomplishments, and education, having lost her fortune, wishes to keep company with a single person."

That by this single person a man is meant, is plain, from her praising her figure, which, if it had been addressed to females, would have been superfluous, perhaps even prejudical.

"A single young lady, thirty years of age, of good family, with 16,000 francs, and a pretty considerable property in moveables, wishes for a legitimate union, *(à s'unir légitimement,)* with a man between thirty and forty-five years of age, who has a situation in some office or possesses some property."

At last here is one who wishes for a legitimate union. But as the word *légitimement* must be placed next to *unir*, to show this legitimacy, it is clear that all the others who have been speaking of union and *unité* without this addition, could not have matrimony in view. We see at least from this example, how far a female with 16,000 francs may be brought, if she *owns* herself thirty years of age.

"A man, sixty-three years of age, in good health, and a widower without children, wishes to become acquainted with a lady, endowed with all the qualities that are generally required of them, in order, perhaps, to offer her his hand, if, upon further acquaintance, their respective moral qualifications inspire them with the hope of living happily together; or, if she should prefer it, merely to unite her interest with his, without any other tie than that of friendship, on which she may safely rely on his part."

To give some idea of the indecent freedoms of the females in France, we shall give the following anecdote:

"In the spring of 1802, Mr. Holcroft received a very polite note from a lady, at whose house he visited, particularly requesting to see him. He went; her maid informed him that her mistress was in the warm bath, but she would announce his arrival. The servant returned, and led him to a kind of closet where her mistress was up to her chin in water. He knew the manners of the place, and that custom had robbed this incident of that impropriety which would have been attached to it in England. What the lady wanted to communicate was, that she had been assured a Frenchman of the name of Fievé had been sent to England to bribe the editors of some journals who had been rather too free in their remarks on the conduct of the first consul. It was with difficulty he could persuade her his interference would be of no avail.

Among shopkeepers, their wives generally attend on and serve the customers; it is agreeable to both parties. The wife dresses herself for exhibition, sits in the shop, and has generally a succession of gallant idlers, (whose wives are acting the same in their own shops,) who come and gossip with them, in the usual routine of tittle tattle, with as much of amorous interlocution as the parties shall think proper. An Englishman whimsically observes that the husband is the sleeping and the wife the active partner. Though there are exceptions in which the husband stays at home and attends business.

In 1559 people were married at the door of the church. When Elizabeth of France, daughter of Henry II. was married to Philip II. of Spain, Eustache de Bellay, bishop of Paris, performed the ceremony at the church door of Notre Dame. Apparently it was then thought indecent for them to grant permission in the church itself for a man and woman to go to bed together. The bride and bridegroom were not allowed to get into the bed until the priest had blessed it, which was a little additional perquisite for him. The priests of Picardy were very troublesome. They pretended that the new married couple ought not, without their permission, to sleep together for the three first nights after their marriage. An *arrêt* appeared in March 19, 1409, prohibiting the Bishop of Amiens and his clergy from exacting any more money from new married persons on that pretence, and it further decreed that they might lawfully sleep together when they pleased without any other permission after the nuptial rites were performed.

The ladies in some parts of France exercise a degree of influence over their husbands which is almost inconceivable; and in Marseilles, in the South of France, that influence is carried to great excess. The women of the lower class are of truly Amazonian race. They have little beauty, but much corporeal strength. It is impossible to conceive females more rough, hardy, and violent; but their rectitude demands the highest encomiums. The wives of the porters, fishermen, &c. have their peculiarities, from their different modes of life; but they all agree in their endeavours to vie with the men in hard labour, and in keeping them in perfect subjection. Whoever wishes to study female government, should betake himself to Sourribes, where he will find a complete female republic, and the men only regarded as slaves. The unmarried women of this class have, notwithstanding the many freedoms they use, much self-government. A young man must first be their acquaintance, their friend, their betrothed, before they will permit him the slightest indulgence. Thus they secure their future power, and they are careful not to let their tenderness influence their conduct. The least contradiction, the slightest neglect, procures his instantaneous dismissal. When a lover has become insupportable to his mistress, she uses no verbal declaration to signify her intention, but, placing a large log of wood before the fire when he is present, nothing more is requisite to inform him he must not appear there again.

Near the City of St. Omer, in France, is the suburb of Haut-pont, inhabited by Flemings, who so strictly intermarry with each other, that the bishop is empowered by the holy see to grant them dispensations to marry within the law of consanguinity prohibited by the church.

ENGLAND.

In England, marriage, taken in the light of a civil contract, the law treats as other contracts. By several statutes a penalty of 100*l.* is inflicted for marrying any persons without banns or licence; but by 26 Geo. III. c. 3, if any person solemnize matrimony without banns or licence obtained from some one having authority to grant the same, or in any other place than a church or chapel, unless by special licence from the Archbishop of Canterbury, he shall be guilty of felony, and transported for 14 years, and the marriage shall be void. Marriages according to the laws of any other country are valid in England, if duly solemnized according to the law of such country. Marriages by licence, where the parties are not twenty-one, must not be without the consent of the father or guardian, or, if they are beyond sea, or insane, or from any other cause incapable of acting, the Chancellor will proceed upon relation in their stead. Marriages cannot be solemnized by persons within the Levitical degrees, but if solemnized, they are not void until sentence is passed by the proper court. To marry an heiress, forcibly, is capital felony.

An English husband and wife are termed *baron* and *feme*, and in law are one person; that is, the very being or legal existence of the woman is suspended during marriage; or, at least, is incorporated and consolidated into that of the husband. A man cannot grant lands to his wife during the coverture, but he may, by his deed, covenant with others for her use, and he may give to her by devise or will. All deeds executed and acts done by the wife during her coverture, are void, except a fine, or the like matter of record, in which case she must be solely and secretly examined, that it may be known whether her act is voluntary. A wife shall not suffer any punishment for committing a base theft in company with and by coercion of her husband. A husband may restrain his wife of her liberty, in case of any gross misbehaviour; but, if he threaten to kill or ill treat her, she may make him find surety of the peace. The husband, by marriage, obtains a freehold in right of his wife, and may make lease thereof for twenty-one years, or three lives. The husband also gains a chattel real, as a term for years, to dispose of, if he please, by grant or lease, in her life-time, or by surviving her; he hath also an absolute gift to chattels personal, in possession of the wife in her own right.

By custom, in London, a wife may carry on a separate trade, and, as such, is liable to the statutes of bankruptcy. If the wife is indebted before her marriage, the husband is bound to pay her debts. The husband is bound to provide his wife necessaries, and, if she contract them, he is obliged to pay for them. A man having issue by his wife, born alive, shall be tenant by the courtesy of all the lands in fee simple, or fee-tail in general, of which she shall be seised. If she survive the husband, she shall have for her dower the third part of all his freehold lands.

In the reign of Edward the First, A. D. 1302, William Paynell, knight, and Margaret, his wife, demanded the third part of the manor of Tarput, as the dower of the said Margaret, after the death of John de Camoys, her first husband, the manor being then in the king's hands. The Attorney General answered, that she ought not to be endowed, because she departed from her husband in his life-time, and lived as an adultress with the said Sir William, and was not reconciled to her husband before his death; and so by the form of the stat. (West. 2, chap. 34.) she ought not to have her dower. The demandants replied, and pleaded a deed of the former husband under his seal, of which the following is a translation.

" To all Christian people to whom these presents may come, John de Camoys, son and heir of Sir Ralf de Camoys, sendeth greeting: —Know, ye, that I have, of my own will delivered and demised to Sir William Paynell, Knt. my wife, Margaret de Camoys, daughter and heir of John Batesden, and that I have also given and granted, and to the said Sir William released and quit-claimed all the goods and chattels which the said Margaret hath, or hereafter may have; and also whatever is mine of the goods and chattels of the said Margaret, with the appurtenances. So that neither I, nor any one in my name can, or may ever hereafter have or claim any power in or over the said Margaret, or her goods, chattels, and appurtenances.—And I will and grant, and by this present writing confirm, that the aforesaid Margaret shall be and remain with the said Sir William. In witness whereof, I have hereunto affixed my seal, &c."

Sir William and his wife then concluded their reply, by saying—"by virtue of which deed, she, the said Margaret, did not live as an adultress with the said William, but as the wife of the said William."

Whereupon the Attorney General demurred, whether the plea of Sir William and his wife was valid in law; and on this the Court gave judgment that she should not be endowed, this being manifest adultery.

The demandant attempted to produce letters of the bishop reciting a purgation of the adultery, but which were not admitted in evidence.

In some countries there has been so much anxiety manifested to promote happiness in the marriage state, that a fee is given to any couple who live together for a certain period without quarrelling; but which may be considered rather as a public honourable testimony of their conduct towards each other, than in any other point of view; and was probably instituted to promote emulation among young married people, in the hope, that, by learning "to bear and forbear," it might lay the foundation of future connubial happiness; and, taken in this light, the founder of the custom at Dunmow, in Essex, deserves credit for his intentions.

There is a custom, when a couple can swear they have lived together for the last year without any discord, wrangling, or opposition of any kind to each other, which entitles them to claim a flitch of bacon from the lord of the manor; and upon their receiving the same they are carried home on the shoulders of their neighbours, with rustic music and acclamations of joy.

At East and West Enborne, in the County of Berks, if a customary tenant die, the widow shall have what the law calls her *Free Bench* in all his copyhold lands, *dum sola et casta fuerit*; that is, while she lives single and chaste; but if she commits incontinency, she forfeits her estate: yet, if she will come into the Court, riding backward upon a black ram, with his tail in her hand, and say the following words, the steward is bound by the custom to re-admit her to her *Free Bench*.

"Here I am,
Riding upon a black ram,
Like a whore as I am;
And for my crincum crancum,
I've lost my bincum bancum;
And for my tail's game,
Have done this worldly shame;
Therefore, I pray you, Mr. Steward,
Let me have my lands again."

WALES.——The lower class of people in Caernarvonshire, Anglesea, and part of Merionethshire, have a mode of courtship very opposite to any practised by most countries, and which, till within these few years, was unheard of in England. The lover generally comes under shadow of the night, and is taken, without any kind of reserve, to the bed of his mistress. Here, as it is generally understood, with part of his clothes on, he breathes his tender passion, and "tells how true he loves."

This custom seems to have originated from the scarcity of fuel, and the disagreeableness of sitting together in the cold weather without a fire. Much has been said of the innocence with which those meetings are conducted; it may be so in some cases, but it is certainly no uncommon thing for a son and heir to be born within two or three months after the marriage ceremony.

To the honour, however, of the Welch gallants, it must be confessed that they very rarely desert the woman who has made them happy; nor does either sex feel any impropriety in the practice to which we have referred. To a stranger, a Welch female would be as reserved as any woman on earth could be; she knows he is not to be trusted; and the most errant clown of her own country would be preferred to a London beau. As wives, they are generally faithful, dutiful, and affectionate. When it is settled that a wedding is to take place, a few days previous to its solemnization, the parents of the parties have what they call a bidding, or meeting of their friends at their separate houses. If they are persons of respectability, the number that attends is prodigious. Where the intended bride lives, great numbers of women and several men make their appearance; the former generally come on horseback, and bring presents, such as cheeses, butter, flour, sugar, tea, &c. The women have an apartment to themselves, where they are entertained with tea; while the men take hearty potations of *cwrw*, and leave such a sum of money as they choose, or can afford. At the bridegroom's it is chiefly men who attend, where, after being entertained in a similar manner, they leave a pecuniary present, and retire. Twenty, thirty, or forty pounds are sometimes collected on such occasions, which helps to establish the young couple in beginning life. On the night previous to the wedding, a few of the bridegroom's friends proceed to the bride's house to see if she is safe, when her friends conceal her for a time, either by dressing her in man's apparel, or by putting her in some obscure place; but, after some pretended difficulty, she is at length discovered, when they sit down, and, after spending the evening merrily, depart home. Next morning they return again and demand the bride, by repeating several lines in Welch poetry. A kind of refusal is made by her father in a similar kind of poetry; but his consent being at last obtained, the girl is mounted on a horse, behind one of her young male friends, who sets off with her at full speed, to the church where the ceremony is to be performed, followed by a numerous concourse of people. The bridegroom is always in readiness to meet her at the church-door, with his attendants, when the clergyman joins them together according to the established ritual, except when he comes to the words, "with my body I thee worship, and with all my worldly goods I thee endow," the bridegroom puts his hand into his pocket, and produces what money he has about him, which he gives with the ring to the clergyman. The latter takes his fee, and delivers the remainder to the bride. After this, the ceremony concludes at the altar in the usual form.

It was the custom formerly for the husband

to make a present to his wife on the morning after the marriage, before she arose out of bed, which presents were considered as her own individual property.

Among the ancient Britons, in very remote times, it was customary to have the women of ten or twelve families, who dwelt under one roof, in common, even to brothers. It is said that Julia, wife to the Emperor Severus, reproaching a Briton with this custom, received the following answer:—"that the Roman ladies ought not to reproach the British ladies on this account, as what the latter did publicly with men of merit, the former did privately with the worst, and sometimes with their slaves."

SCOTLAND.——There was a custom in this country formerly that savours so much of brutality and tyranny, that it seems almost incomprehensible to the present polished state of society, that it should have ever obtained the sanction of a law; but we have it from undoubted authority, that Evenus III. sixteenth King of Scotland, made a law, that the king should have the first night after marriage of all noblemen's daughters; and noblemen and heritors of lands should have the same freedom with their tenants' and vassals' daughters, and that both wives and daughters of every subject should be common to the king and his nobles. The law giving the first night after marriage to the landlord was in being till the time of Malcolm III. whose queen, called St. Margaret, procured the abolition of so wicked a law, and in lieu thereof they were to have a mark of silver to redeem their chastity.

The practice of espousing stepmothers in this country appears to have been prevalent so late as the eleventh century, and is supposed by Lord Hailes to have originated from motives of interest, that the estate might be exonerated from the payment of a jointure.

By the Scottish laws the crime of incest is punished by the decapitation of the guilty parties.

THE QUAKERS.——Throughout the civilized world there is not perhaps any sect who use so little pomp and ceremony in their marriages as the Quakers, and perhaps in no sect are there so few instances of the violation of the marriage vow, nor have they on record a single instance of divorce. They use no oaths, but merely the simple assertion, before witnesses, that they will live together—and they use the same forms in every country which they inhabit. When a young couple has agreed to live together in the holy state of matrimony, they stand up in the meeting when there is a congregation, before whom they mutually declare their intention of marrying, and whatever agreement is made between them they insert upon a parchment decorated with other devices, according to the fancy or circumstances of the party, which agreement is then signed and witnessed by as many persons present as choose. It is then given to the woman, and record is made in the books of the society, which renders the marriage complete.

THE JEWS,

IN all their rites and festivals, have more ceremonies than any nation on the earth, and their marriage ceremony is far more impressive than those practised by the Christians.—It is very customary among them for the bride and bridegroom to be betrothed six months, sometimes twelve, before their marriage, as may be be agreed on by the parties, during which time the bridegroom visits his bride, but without any further commerce with her.

On the day fixed for the celebration of the nuptials, the bride and bridegroom are conducted to the place appointed by the parties or their friends; the bridegroom by the men, and the bride by the women; where there are generally assembled all or most of their relations and friends, as they generally invite a great many, being obliged to have at least ten men present, otherwise the marriage is null and void. When all the company are assembled, and the priest and reader of the synagogue is come, the ceremony is performed in the following manner.

A velvet canopy is brought into the room supported by four long poles, under which the bridegroom and bride are led in the following order: the bridegroom being supported by a friend on each side, and the bride by two female friends in the same manner, (which four are always, if living or in the way, the parents of the couple; otherwise the two nearest relations, with their wives,) having her face covered with a veil, in token of female modesty. The couple are then placed opposite to each other under the canopy; the priest takes a glass of wine in his hand, and repeats as follows: "Blessed art thou, O Lord our God, king of the universe, the Creator of the fruit of the vine. —Blessed art thou, O Lord our God, king of the universe, who hath sanctified us with thy commandments, and hath forbidden us fornication, and hath forbidden to us the betrothed, but hath allowed unto us *those that* are married unto us, by the *means of* the canopy and of the wedding-ring. Blessed art thou, O Lord, who art the sanctifier of thy people Israel, by the means of the canopy and of the wedlock." Then the bride and bridegroom drink of the wine, and the latter puts a ring upon the bride's finger, saying, in presence of those who stand round the canopy, "Behold, thou art betrothed unto me with this ring, according to the rites of Moses and of Israel." The instruments of the marriage contract are read, which specifies that the bridegroom A. B. doth agree to take the bride C. D. as his lawful wife, according to the laws of Moses and Israel; and that he will keep, maintain, honour, and cherish, her, according to the manner of all the Jews, who honour, keep, maintain, and cherish, their wives; that he will keep her in clothing decently, according to the manner of the world. It likewise specifies what sum he will settle on her in case of his death, and by which he obliges his heirs, executors, administrators, &c. to pay the same to her of the first produce of his effects.

The priest and reader then each drink a glass of wine; and, after a prayer, the bride and bridegroom drink of the wine: the empty glass is then laid on the ground, and the bridegroom with his foot breaks it, the intent and meaning of which is to remind them of death, to whose power mortals must yield sooner or later, and therefore to induce them to live in such a manner as not to fear its approach. This being over, all who are present cry out *mozul tour*, i. e. may it turn out happily. The ceremony is then concluded.

The Jews from the earliest period have been very strict in their laws respecting marriage; and it was perhaps necessary that they should be so, to prevent the probability of their falling into idolatry by taking to wife the females of the heathen nations through which they had to pass into Judea; and when that danger was over, and they were safely settled in the land promised to their forefathers, they framed laws equally strict for the guidance of the females of their own nation, and to preserve the lineal descendants of their families free from stain. We extract the following from *Josephus's Antiquities of the Jewish nation.*

"Let those who are full of years to be married match themselves with virtuous virgins, and such as are born of honest parents. And he that will not take a virgin to wife, let him not abuse himself with one that is married to another man, lest he breed discontent and sorrow in her first husband. Let not free men match themselves with such as are servants; no, not although they be moved thereunto by love, for it is a thing worthy, and befitting honour, to surmount a man's affection. Let no man meddle with a harlot, for the children shall be of a free heart, and addressed in virtue, if they be begotten by a free father and mother. If any one that is married for a virgin be afterwards found to the contrary, let her be brought before the judge, and let him produce all the signs that he can, and let the new married wife's cause be defended by her father, or brother, or by them who, next unto them, shall seem to be her next in blood; and if the damsel be found to have committed no crime, let her return and dwell with him that hath accused her, who cannot any more refuse her, except she give him great occasions, whereunto she cannot contradict. But he that, without cause and rashly, shall accuse and slander his wife, he shall be punished with thirty-nine stripes; and, in way of amends, shall pay fifty sicles to her father. But if it be proved that she hath been deflowered, and hath been common, then shall she be stoned to death, for that she hath not chastely conserved her virginity till the time of her lawful marriage; and, if she be of the race of the Priests, she shall be burned alive.

"If any man have two wives, the one of which he holdeth in great honour and amity, either for love, or by reason of her beauty, and that the other be not in the like condition and estimate; if the son of her that is best beloved demandeth to have the prerogative of the elder, which is two portions of that which cometh to all the rest by the father's patrimony, (for so much import our ordinances), and challengeth the same, by reason that his father more dearly loveth his mother than the other, let it not be granted him. For it is an act against justice, that the eldest should be deprived of that which appertaineth unto him, because his mother's condition is inferior to that of the others, by reason of his father's affection.

"Whosoever shall violate a maiden, being betrothed to another man, if by persuasion she hath consented to lie with him, let her die with him; for they are both of them equally guilty of sin; the man, because he hath persuaded the maiden to consent to an insufferable dishonour; and the maid, for suffering herself to be overcome, either from inclination, or for the sake of lucre. But if, meeting her alone, he shall enforce her, and she have none to succour her hard by, let him die alone.

"He that shall deflower the virgin that is unmarried, he shall take her to wife; but if he condescend not to the father, to entertain her in wedlock, he shall pay fifty sicles, for amends of the inquiry.

"If any man pretend to separate himself from his wife for certain causes, such as ordinarily happen amongst married couples, let him confirm it in writing, that he will never more entertain her again; and so may she marry again unto another, and refuse the former husband: and if it happen that she were evil entreated by the second, or that, he being dead, the first would take her again in marriage, it is not lawful for the wife to return unto him.

"If the brother of him that is deceased without issue take to wife her whom his deceased brother had married, and that the son which was born by this second wedlock beareth his name, let him be brought up as the successor of his inheritance, (which thing is granted for public profit sake, to the end that families should not come to ruin, and that the goods should remain to those of the same kindred.) Furthermore, it is allowed for the comfort of afflicted women that they may be joined in marriage with the next akin of their first husband. But if the brother will not take her to wife, she shall repair unto the Senate, and make this protestation, That the brother of her deceased husband will not entertain her, (although she had desired to remain in that line, and bring forth infants unto him,) protesting, that by him only the memory of her deceased husband was dishonoured. And when the Senate shall have examined the cause why he estrangeth himself from this marriage his excuse shall be allowed of, how great or slight consequence soever it be; and then shall the widow unloose his shoe, and spit in his face, and tell him, that he hath deservedly suffered these things, in that he hath injured the memory of his dead brother. And thus shall he depart out of the Court, being defamed for his whole life time, and the woman may marry whomsoever she list.

"If any man take a virgin prisoner, or such a one as hath been already married, and be desirous to take her to his wife, it is not lawful for him to touch or approach her before such time as she hath been shaved, and, having put on her mourning apparel, hath bewailed her parents or friends slain in battle; but after she hath in this sort assuaged her sorrow, she may afterwards addict herself to mirth and marriage. For it is a matter both honest and just, that he that entertaineth her, to have issue by her, should condescend unto her will, in all that wherein he might gratify her, and that he should not alone addict himself to the pursuit of his pleasure.—When the thirty days of mourning shall be expired, (for that time is sufficient for the wife to bewail her friends in,) then may she hearken after marriage. And if, after he hath had his pleasure with her, it fortune that he mislike her, and will not accept her for his wife, he can no more make her his slave, but she may go whithersoever she pleaseth, for that she beareth her liberty with her."

SPAIN.

THE Spaniards, from public opinion, from religious principles, and from national taste, are always inclined to marry early. Some privileges are besides annexed to the married state; the slightest evidence is deemed sufficient to criminate a bachelor, whereas it is necessary to bring the strongest evidence against a married man, unless his wife be the complainant. In the Spanish dominions, females are reckoned marriageable at twelve, and males at fourteen; and nothing is more common in this country than for a husband and his wife's ages together not to amount to thirty. Congeniality of sentiment and disposition is never consulted in their matches; passion is mistaken for affection, and that important tie which is to form the future happiness or misery of life, is entered into with as little reflection as if it were only to remain binding for a single day. The precipitancy of entering into the married state proceeds, in a great measure, from the nature of the Spanish laws, which, in this respect, give the parent too little authority over his children. It is true that the Spanish law fixes the period of majority at twenty-five, and till that age the consent of parents is necessary to constitute a legal marriage; but this salutary provision is frequently evaded and rendered nugatory; as a boy of fourteen and a girl of twelve years old, who long to be united in indissoluble bonds, can demand, as the law prescribes, the consent of their parents. If the morals, education, or manners of either of the parties be deemed exceptionable, the parents have a right to refuse their consent; but this refusal, which in another country would be sufficient to render any anterior contract null and void, here only opens a door for a vexatious and scandalous process between a child and its parents; and the law, so far from aiding the parental authority, forces them to furnish a marriage portion to their disobedient children according to their circumstances, and likewise to pay the expences of the suit for obtaining the same. The only plea admitted in those courts for a parent withholding his consent to the marriage of his child, is inferiority of birth; but, if he fail to establish this point, neither the bad conduct of the party, disparity of age, or inequality in point of fortune, will prevent the tribunal from ordering the immediate celebration of the marriage. In a country like Spain, where hereditary greatness is alone held in estimation, it is easy to perceive the ruinous consequences and implacable hatred which must necessarily flow from this just and impolitic law.

There is another and a more simple mode, by which a child may elude parental restraint in any of the Spanish dominions, but which is nevertheless seldom resorted to. It is sufficient to constitute a legal marriage, if the parties declare in the presence of a priest that they take each other for husband and wife. When this formality is complied with, neither the non-publication of banns, nor the opposition of parents, can prevent the marriage. It is true, the civil law in this respect is opposite to the canonical law, and proscribes those sorts of contracts; but as they inflict no penalty upon the offending parties, and as parents can only seek redress by a tedious prosecution, they have hardly an alternative between pardoning or finally throwing off their offending offspring.

Domestic unhappiness so evident in this country is, we think, justly attributable to too early marrying. To the impetuosity and effervescence of passion succeeds the calm of reflection; and a difference of character and disposition soon begins to manifest itself, which was never dreamt of by the young lovers, that frequently embitters every succeeding moment of their lives. They endeavour to support an appearance of cordiality, while their hearts are filled with mutual hatred; and fidelity becomes a farce, which they strive to get rid of as soon as possible. The children, who have continually before their eyes the infidelity of their parents, and the intrigues of their mother, from their most tender infancy, soon learn to despise every moral obligation; and thus vice, becoming hereditary as it were, is transmitted from generation to generation.

The blind protection afforded by the Spanish laws to females, in opposition to their husbands, is another cause of the unhappiness of marriages. No being can be nore unfortunate than a Spanish husband whose wife is jealous, dissolute, or peevish. If tormented by the first of these passions, she readily finds access to the civil and ecclesiastical authority, which in such cases usually evince a disposition implicity to believe every thing that a heated and angry imagination can suggest against her husband. The most common complaints are, that the husband keeps a mistress; that he spends all his fortune in dissipation, while she and her family are in want of the common comforts of life, &c. No proof is required of these or similar assertions; she is believed on her simple word. The husband, in such cases, according to the rank he holds in society, is either cited to appear, in order that he may receive a severe reprimand, or he is instantly, and without further inquiry, thrown into prison, where he generally continues till his wife solicits his enlargement. If the husband, on the contrary complain of the conduct of his wife, she has only to bring forward an accusation that attacks his honour, and the poor husband is condemned to silence and greater discretion; happy even if he is not subjected to the penalty which ought to have been incurred by his wife.

A Spanish husband cannot undertake a journey without the consent of his wife, and making a certain provision for her during his absence; if he do not return within the time limited, the judge, on the first application of the wife, immediately orders his return, were he even in Chili or California; whether his business be terminated or not, the wife has only to speak, the husband must obey.

Military officers, and those employed in civil capacities, are forced to appropriate a large portion of their pay, never less than two-thirds thereof, to the maintainance of their wives; and if one half of this be not done voluntarily, the treasury has the power of retaining it for their use.

Notwithstanding what has been said, it would be uncandid not to acknowledge that many Spanish families live in the greatest harmony, and afford examples of every domestic virtue to their children. There is an habitual air of frankness and candour in this people, which, judging from appearance, would lead us to believe that in no country was filial obedience more respected. Every evening and morning, the Spanish children of every rank and condition solicit and receive on their knees the parental benediction; and the ceremony is repeated through the day, upon their return after a long absence. The general mode of address from children to their parents is also marked with the greatest humility. But such external homage proceeds less from sentiment than from habit and fashion, and may justly be ranked among the absurd ceremonies so numerous among the Spaniards.

The Spanish *Cortejos* are similar to the Italian *Cecisbeo's;* they attend upon the lady wherever she goes; some are attendant upon her when she goes to church, others when she pays visits; one presides over this amusement, another over that; nor is it at all reputable for a lady to change her *Cortejo*, even retaining them, if they can, until old age. Sometimes, when a lady is apt to change, she will not easily be provided with another *Cortejo*.

Marriages in Valencia are attended with an enormous expence, which is the more preposterous, as few of the young women have any fortune. On those occasions Spanish vanity displays an extraordinary magnificence.

For some days previous to the ceremony, the gowns, linen, &c. &c. the jewels intended to be presented to her, and the presents she has received, are publicly displayed; these matters are so carefully shown, indeed in so studied a manner, that a stranger might enter the room where the bride's paraphernalia is, and fancy he was in a milliner's or jeweller's shop. To different companies as they come in, a female relation enumerates the articles; tells what places the stuffs came from; carefully points out what belonged to the bride, what she owes to the tenderness or vanity of her lover, and what is given to her by her parents, whose generosity is always the greater from their knowing the public will be acquainted therewith. The luxury in the wedding-feasts, in the ball that follows, and the equipages which are provided, is enormous and expensive in the extreme.

An opposite practice sometimes prevails among the middling people, which brings to mind the golden age, when our first parents had nothing more than a hillock or turf of grass for their bed. After the ceremony, the bride returns to her father's house, where she remains all the day with her friends and companions. At midnight, the bridegroom, accompanied by his relations, goes for her and takes her to the yard belonging to the house, where the nuptial bed has been prepared in an arbour of flowers. In the morning, they return to their father's house, where breakfast is prepared for the guests, who soon meet, and the girls present the bride with a cradle made of twigs. The day is concluded with various diversions.

Any person travelling through Spain, and remarking the customs in all cases respecting the conduct of one sex to the other, would be led to suppose, that the laws enforcing those customs were made by females, as they are all of them so evidently in their favour. Bourgoing, in his *Travels through Spain*, mentions the following very arbitrary law. Every girl, who has obtained the age of twelve, may compel a young man to marry her, provided he has reached his fourteenth year, and she can prove that he has anticipated the rights of a husband with her; that he has promised her his hand, or given her to understand that he wished her to become his wife. These proofs are adduced before an ecclesiastical vicar. If the woman affirm that the man has been intimate with her, and he admit the fact, he is then bound to espouse her; if he deny the charge, she is bound to substantiate it by proofs; and for this purpose it is enough that some neighbours assert their having seen them together at an unseasonable hour. A present of a ring or trinket, but above all a love-letter, though even the word marriage be not mentioned in it, is considered sufficient proof to enable the girl to claim the husband. It is difficult to say in what spirit such laws were enacted. Was it meant that one sex should be put on its guard against the seductions of the other, even at the tenderest age? or did the legislature wish it to be understood, that the encouragement must be given to marriage, even at the risk of forming many unhappy unions? Be this as it may, no sooner does the complainant apply to the vicar, than he orders the defendant immediately into prison, where he remains till the cause is decided. If the vicar pronounce that the marriage ought to take place the prisoner is not liberated until after the celebration thereof. The desire of recovering his liberty for the present, frequently induces him to make a sacrifice of it for life; but it may very easily be imagined, that a union thus imposed does not sit easy long upon him who has been constrained to enter into it.

Among other rules of the Spanish Court, the following were drawn up by Philip II. specifying the etiquette to be observed by the King in his nocturnal visits to the Queen: When the king comes out of his chamber at night to go into the queen's, he must wear his shoes like slippers, his black coat upon his shoulders, his *broquel*, or buckler, fastened under his arm, and his bottle fastened with a string to his other arm;—but you must not think this bottle holds drink to quench thirst; no, it is for quite a different purpose, which you must guess. With all these accoutrements the king has besides in one hand a long rapier, in the other a dark lantern; and in this manner he must go alone to the queen's chamber. The hour at which she was to retire to bed was nine in winter, and ten in summer. The Spaniards have a custom, during courtship, of exercising flagellation upon themselves, and, if possible, to let some of their blood fly upon the lady of their affection, which permission is looked upon as a particular mark of their favour. At the bull-fights the lover shews his courage to gain the approbation of his mistress, she generally being present; and, when he has vanquished his adversary, he presents his sword to her, which she salutes. A cavalier, when attending a lady, must not offer her his arm, nor take hold of hers; but, wrapped up in his cloak, he presents his elbow to the lady.— Favoured lovers were not allowed to kiss their mistresses; the greatest caress was permission to clasp and gently press the arms of the fair; and one of the greatest gallantries was to hold a handkerchief to the eyes, mouth, or heart.

The Spanish gentry also serenade their mistresses, which is by the lover playing on and singing to a guitar, accompanied by other instruments, under her window. They sometimes perform all night, and it is often very pleasing.

The marriage rites of the PORTUGUESE are very similar to those of the Spaniards; but, as they are of a more reserved and jealous nature than their neighbours, they do not admit of those amatory customs which are so frequent among the Spaniards. It is said to be a principal amusement among the married ladies of Portugal, on gala or festival days, to sit at their windows, where they display all their finery; and during the carnival, they amuse themselves with pelting the passers-by with stones, dirt, and squirting water; one lady had a squirt made large enough to knock down a person with the water discharged therefrom.

ROME, VENICE, GREECE, &c.

THERE is a very excellent foundation established at Rome, for the purpose of portioning out poor girls. A girl is at liberty to sue for her portion, without having a husband. If her request is countenanced, she receives only a written assurance of 30, 40, or 50, scudi, but the money is paid the day after marriage. All the girls thus portioned must, on a certain day, and in a peculiar dress, form a procession, in order to show their obligations before the eyes of every body; whence many a good girl is debarred from having a husband.

Notwithstanding the fondness of amorous intrigue so prevailing among the Italian ladies, their favourite passion is treated in a methodical manner only at Rome. How would it be possible to procure husbands to such an immense number of poor girls in a city which abounds with unmarried inhabitants, were not all the powers of art and stratagem exerted! Many foreign artists have fallen into these snares, and got a wife against every expectation. Accidents of this nature happen daily; parents permit their daughters to look all day out of one of the windows, and, whilst in other countries love affairs are concealed from the knowledge of their mothers, these become in Rome the confidants of their daughters, and assist them with their advice, ripened by experience. When the girl is looking out of the window in her fine dress, it makes an impression upon a man passing by, and he wishes for her acquaintance: he may know whether his wishes will be granted by staring in the girl's face, and greeting her at some distance, in order that the neighbours may take no notice of it. If she do not thank him, he has no hopes; but if the compliment be returned, it is a good sign, and he may boldly venture a letter. Time and place are appointed for a conversation; and though the lover be unable to support himself, and still less a wife, or his rank be above any thought of such an alliance, still will the "beggar girl" plainly ask him, "Will you marry me?" If the gallant finds the proposal againt his liking, the girl, in concert with her mother, tries every art possible, and often the two lovers are surprised, by the parent and other witnesses, in a posture which is not equivocal. Then the dupe has no other choice than to pay a large sum of money fixed by law, to embrace matrimony, or go to the gallies.

Notwithstanding the laxity of moral so prevalent at this time in Italy, and the little attention that is paid to the fidelity of the marriage vow, it is considered so sacred by the ancient Romans, and as a tie of so indissoluble a nature, that for five hundred and twenty years after the foundation of the city, a divorce was not known to have happened; this offers a strong proof of the private virtues of the inhabitants of the ancient "mistress of the world."

It is a common practice among the Italians of the present day to allow their grown daughters to sleep in the same bed with their parents, which is the more improper and indelicate, as from the warmth of the climate they can bear but a very slight covering on them in bed, and they are in consequence very frequently in a state of nudity.

It is customary among the Italians, when there is more than one son in a family, only the elder may marry, and take the title and estate; the others have inferior pensions assigned them. The same rule is observed with daughters: several are thrown into convents in order to make a large fortune to spare for the favourite; on which account parents are obliged to have a strict eye over them, that they do not frustrate their designs by intriguing.

The Cecisbeat, a custom observed all over Italy, is no where carried to a more ridiculous and extravagant degree than in Genoa. With the day of the nuptials ceases every public intercourse between husband and wife; they must not even be seen together, neither walking, nor at the playhouse, nor in company; in short, no where but at home. In other cities many a husband puts himself above that foolish usage, out of love to his spouse, and has nothing else to fear, than to be looked upon as an unfashionable husband; but here the most united couple must not think of such a thing. To be forsaken by all friends, derided by enemies, insulted by the mob, are unavoidable consequences, if they are ever seen together in public.

In some of the Italian States, marriages are not permitted between persons professing different religions. A woman of 40 years of age is not permitted to be united to a man under 30; if she exceeds 40, her husband must at least be 35; a man above 60 is not to marry a woman whose age is less than 30. A widow is not allowed to alter her condition in less than six months after her widowhood.

In VENICE, they have a very singular ceremony which takes place every year on Ascension Day, and is called the Marriage of the Doge of Venice to the Sea. Early on the morning of that day, all the senators, dressed in their robes, assemble together in a large apartment in the Doge's palace, where musicians attend with all kinds of music. About ten o'clock his Serene Highness comes from his palace preceded by the music and banner; on one side of him is the Pope's nuncio, and on the other the bishop or patriarch of Venice. The senators, foreign ambassadors, and great numbers of the nobility in their black robes, follow, the music playing before them; in this order they walk to the seaside, where a magnificient vessel called the Busentoro, is waiting to receive them. This is esteemed the richest vessel in the whole world; it is most curiously adorned with the richest sculpture, gilding, painting, &c. that it can possibly have, and will contain upwards of 400 people. At the head of the poop is a very rich chair of state, in which sits the Doge with the Nuncio and Patriarch on either side of him; the nobility, &c. sit on gilt benches in the other parts of the vessel. There is a kind of temporary bridge made for the purpose for them to embark with, along which they all walk in procession after the Doge, on board the Busentoro. When they are placed in their respective seats, a signal is given to the slaves who are to row the vessel, of which there are forty, twenty on each side, under hatches, a person on the deck steering; they then move forward in a majestic manner, attended by the gondolas of the ambassadors, &c. which, for this occasion, are superbly gilt and ornamented; also several other larger vessels, called piottas, and some large gallies with ensigns and banners displayed, which together make a grand appearance. In this manner they proceed about two miles up the Laguna; when arrived at a certain place, they all stop. The Doge then rises from his chair of state, goes to the side of the vessel, and throws a gold ring into the sea, repeating the following words: *Despondamus te, mare, in signum perpetui domini;* which is, "We espouse thee, O Sea! as a token of our perpetual dominion over thee." At the close of this part of the ceremony all the gallies fire their guns, and the music continues to play. On their voyage back they stop at a small island, where they go to church, and high mass is there celebrated. They then return in the same order they at first set out.

Mr. Trapp, in his *Pictures of Italy*, mentions a most flagitious custom in this state, and one most repugnant to the moral feeling of this country. We shall transcribe it in his own words:—"The girls of pleasure are another class of beings who receive the protection of government. They belong to the entertainments of the Carnival, which could not do well without them. Most part of these unfortunate females are sold by their parents in their tender infancy. These make a regular agreement with lovers, or dealers in virginity. It is done before a notary public, stands valid in every court of justice, and specifies a time when Miss is to be yielded up, upon paying a stipulated sum. The usual price is from one to two hundred zechins. This, however, is a mere pretence, as their parents keep the money, and leave their daughter in a brothel. These nymphs observe most strictly their fasts, go daily to mass, and have their special tutelar saint, under whose auspices they exercise their profession with a good conscience."

GREECE.—The Grecian woman of the Archipelago are generally while single chaste, and when married faithful and affectionate to their husbands, possessing a certain austerity of conduct which repels all attempts at Asiatic voluptuousness. After the death of the husband of their choice, they very rarely make a new engagement; on the contrary, they seem to labour under existence when they have lost their partner, passing much of their time in tears and the most pathetic lamentations.

Among the ancient Greeks it was common for them to indulge their love unconfined and promiscuous; because, forbidden by no human authority, it was permitted without controul. The first that restrained this liberty was Cecrops, who, having raised himself to be king over that people, afterwards called the Athenians, amongst many other useful institutions, introduced that of marriage. In short, no sooner had the Greeks in general entered into a state of civilization, than they found it necessary, by marriage, and other good rules of manners, to restrain the unruly passions of men.

Marriage was very honourable in several of the Grecian commonwealths, it being as much encouraged by their laws as the abstaining from it was discountenanced, and in some places even punished. The strength of states consisting in the number of their inhabitants, those that refused to contribute to their increase were thought to be very cold in their affections to their country.

The Lacedæmonians are very remarkable for their severity against those that deferred marrying, as well as those who abstained therefrom. No man among them could live single beyond the time limited by their lawgiver, without incurring several penalties; as, first, the magistrates commanded such, once every winter, to run round the Public Forum quite naked, and, to increase their shame, they sang a song, the words of which aggravated their crime, and exposed them to ridicule.

Another of their punishments was the being excluded from those exercises in which, according to the Spartan custom, young virgins contended naked. A third penalty was inflicted upon a certain solemnity, wherein the women dragged them round the altar, beating them all the time with their fists. They were also deprived of that respect and observance which the younger were accustomed to pay to their elders; therefore, says Plutarch, no man found fault with what was said to Dercyllidas, a great captain, and one that had commanded armies, who, coming into the place of the assembly, a young man, instead of rising and making room, told him, "Sir, you must not expect that honour from me, though young, which cannot be returned to me by a child of yours when I am old."

To these we may add the Athenian law, whereby all that were commanders, orators, or entrusted with any public office, were to be married, and have children, and estates in land, which were looked on as so many pledges of their good behaviour, without which they thought it dangerous to commit to them the management of public trusts.

Polygamy was not commonly tolerated in Greece, for marriage was thought to be a conjunction of one man with one woman. When Herodotus reports that Anaxandridas the Spartan had two wives, he remarks that it was contrary to the custom of Sparta. The rest of the Grecian cities herein agree with the Lacedemonians, only upon some emergent occasions: when the men had been destroyed by war or some other calamity, toleration was granted for marrying more than one wife.

The time of marriage was not the same in all places; the Spartans were not permitted to marry till they were arrived at their full strength, though we are not informed what was the exact number of years they were confined to; yet it appears from one of Lycurgus's sayings, that both men and women were limited in this particular, that the children might be strong and vigorous. The Athenian laws are said to have ordered that men should not marry under thirty-five years of age; but this depended upon the humour of every law-giver. Aristotle thought thirty-seven a good age, Plato and Hesiod thirty. Some of the old Athenian laws permitted women to marry at twenty-six, Aristotle at eighteen, Hesiod at fifteen, &c. The time or season most proper for marriage was, according to the Athenians, in the winter months, especially January. The most convenient season was when there was a conjunction of the sun and moon, at which time they celebrated the marriage of the gods.

Most of the Grecians thought it scandalous to marry within certain degrees of consanguinity. Hermione, in his play of Euripides, speaks of the custom of brethrens marrying their sisters with no less detestation than of sons marrying their mothers, or fathers their daughters. The Lacedemonians were forbidden to marry any of their kindred, whether in the direct degree of ascent or descent; but a collateral degree hindered them not. They frequently allowed marriages between those that had the same mother and different fathers.

Most of the Grecian states, especially those that made any figure, required their citizens should match with none but citizens, for they looked upon the freedom of their cities as too great a privilege to be granted upon easy terms to foreigners, or their children: hence we find the Athenian laws sentencing the children of such matches to perpetual slavery. They also had a law, that if a foreigner married a free-woman of Athens, it should be lawful for any person to call him to account before the magistrates called *Thesmothetæ*, where, if he were convicted, they sold him for a slave, and all his goods were confiscated, and the third part thereof given to the accuser. The same penalty was inflicted upon persons marrying foreign women to citizens, by pretending they were their own daughters, save that the sentence of slavery was changed into that of ignominy, whereby they were deprived of their voice in public assemblies, and most other privileges as citizens.

But these laws were not always in force; sometimes the necessity of the times so far prevailed, that the children of strange women enjoyed all the rights of citizens.

Virgins were not allowed to marry without the consent of their parents. Even men were not permitted to marry without their father's consent. When virgins had no fathers, their brothers disposed of them; if no brothers, their grandfathers disposed of them. Sometimes husbands on their death-beds would betroth their wives to others. Persons to be married plighted their troth to each other or their relations. Ovid makes the next ceremony after betrothing, to be the virgin's oath to her lover. The ceremony in promising fidelity to each other was to kiss and give the right hand, which was the usual form of ratifying all agreements.

The Thebans had a custom for lovers to plight their faith at the altar of Iolaüs, who was a lover of Hercules, and assisted him in his labours, and was therefore supposed to preside over love affairs.

In the primitive ages, women were married without portions from their relations; as their husbands usually purchased them, his presents to her relations was called the woman's *dowry.* In process of time the men received dowries with their wives. But Lycurgus, partly to prevent wives domineering over their husbands, and partly that men should not marry from any but personal properties, and that no woman's poverty should hinder her of a husband, quite banished the giving of dowries with wives out of Sparta. Heiresses had the privilege of insisting that their husbands should sleep with them at least thrice in every month. When there were any orphan virgins without portions, he that was next of kin was under obligation to marry them himself, or settle a portion on her according to her rank; if there were several of equal consanguinity, they each contributed an equal proportion. If there were more than one virgin, the nearest kinsman was obliged to marry or portion one of them, and, upon his refusal, any person who chose to take it up might cite him before the archon, when he was fined 1000 drachms, which money was consecrated to Juno, the goddess of marriage. When the daughters of eminent men had neither relations nor property to provide for them, the state frequently portioned them; an instance whereof we have in the two daughters of Aristides, to each of which the city gave 300 drachms as a marriage portion. Heirs were obliged to maintain the wives of those whose estates they inherited.

If a man's estate were confiscated, the wife's dowry was secured to her. If a married woman died without having children, her dowry was returned to those that endowed her, the intention of the dower being to support the children, and her sons had a right to their mother's dowry in her life-time, provided they allowed her a sufficient maintenance when they were of age.

The Athenian virgins were presented to Diana, and when they were upon the point of marriage, made offerings to obtain leave to retire from her train. At Troezen the virgins were obliged to consecrate their hair to Hippolytus, the son of Theseus, who died for his chastity, before they entered the marriage state.

The house where the nuptials were celebrated was decked with garlands, a pestle was tied at the door, a servant carried a sieve, the bride herself carrying a vessel wherein was parched barley, to shew her readiness to attend to household affairs. The bride was usually conducted in a chariot from her father's to her husband's house in the evening, that time being chose to conceal her blushes. She was placed in the middle, her husband and one of his most intimate friends being one on each side; if they had been married any time, the fetching her devolved upon the bridegroom's friend. They were attended by singers and dancers, and the axletree of the carriage on which they rode was burnt, to denote that the bride was not to return.

The Rhodians had a peculiar custom of sending for the bride by the public crier. When they arrived at the bridegroom's house, they found a sumptuous entertainment prepared for them, the intent of which was to make the marriage public, and invite all their friends thereto, who were to be witnesses of the marriage, and to shew respect to the gods. During the time of their entertainment, a boy, covered with thorn boughs and acorns, brought a basket full of bread, and sang, *I have left the worst and found the better;* signifying how much the married state was preferable to the single. When the dances were ended, the couple was conducted to the marriage bed; in the same room there was generally placed an extra side-bed, and before they went to bed the bride washed her feet in some water, which was brought by a boy very nearly allied to one of the parties; they were then conducted to bed by the light of several torches, one not being thought sufficient; round one of the torches the mother of the bride tied her hair lace, which she took from her daughter's hair for that purpose. The married couple being alone, they were obliged, by the laws of Athens, to eat a quince between them, thereby intimating that their conversation ought to be pleasant and agreeable. During this time young persons of both sexes sang and danced at the door to drown the maiden's complaints; the songs consisted of the praises of the bride and bridegroom, with wishes for their mutual happiness: they came again in the morning, and saluted them with morning songs.

The Grecian laws concerning divorces were different in many places. The Cretans allowed a man to divorce his wife when he was apprehensive of too large a family. The Athenians likewise permitted divorces upon very slight occasions, but it was not permitted without a bill specifying the reason of their separation, which the magistrate must see and approve. The Athenian women were allowed to separate from their husbands upon any just ground of complaint; but they were under the necessity of appearing in person and publicly exhibiting their complaint to the archon, that by so doing their husband might have an opportunity of seeing and prevailing on them to return. Plutarch relates that Hipparete, the wife of Alcibiades, being a virtuous woman and very fond of her husband, was at last induced, from his debauched life and continual entertainment of courtezans, to leave him and retire to her brother Callias's house. Alcibiades still continued his loose manner of living; but his wife being obliged, before she could obtain a divorce, personally to appear before the magistrate, her husband came in, took her away by force, and carried her home through the forum, where she remained with him till her death, no one daring to interfere.

It was not unusual to dissolve the marriage tie by mutual consent, in which case the parties were at liberty to dispose of themselves afterwards as each thought proper. Nor was it unusual in some parts of Greece to borrow each other's wives, for we are told that Socrates lent his wife Xantippe to Alcibiades. Lycurgus thought that freely imparting their wives to each other was the best way of preventing jealousy, ridiculing those who thought the violation of their bed an insupportable injury, supposing that children were not so much the property of their parents as of the state, in which all had an interest.

Adultery was punished more or less as the crime was considered more or less heinous in different places. They punished by the loss of sight; Zelucus, their lawgiver, being very strict in punishing adultery, and having caught his son in the act, was, for a long time, inexorable, till at last the importunity of the people so far prevailed on him to mitigate the sentence, that he consented the youth should lose one of his eyes and himself one, thereby giving a memorable example of justice and mercy. At Gartyn in Crete adulterers were covered with wool, to denote the effeminacy of their tempers, and in that dress carried through the city to the magistrate's house, who deprived them of nearly all their privileges, and rendered them incapable of taking any part in public affairs.

The Athenian punishments seem to have been arbitary and at the will of the magistrate; whence we find Hippomenes, one of Codrus's posterity, pronouncing a very odd sentence upon his own daughter Limone, and the man caught in adultery with her. They were yoked to a chariot till the man died; afterward the woman was shut up with a horse, and they were both starved to death. Draco and Solon left adulterers at the mercy of any man who caught them in the act. A man that ravished a free women was fined one hundred drachms; one that enticed a free woman twenty, or, as some say, two hundred, it being thought a greater crime to corrupt the mind; he that forced a free virgin must pay one thousand or marry her. Plutarch tells us, that any person, detecting his sister or daughter in this crime, might sell her for a slave. Adultresses were never after permitted to adorn or dress themselves finely; for, in case they so appeared in public, any one might disrobe and beat them, but not so as to cause death; they also underwent the same punishment if they entered any of the temples; a husband was not allowed to cohabit with bis wife after her detection, under pain of ignominy; but persons who prostituted women were punished with death. The Greeks did not think so hardly of concubinage, as we find it was generally practised among then; yet it appears that concubines and harlots were mostly foreigners.

There was a law among the Athenians, that none but men should practice midwifery, it being forbidden to women and slaves, until a free women, having disguised herself in man's apparel, after practising the art for some time, and from her extensive practice exciting the jealousy of the physicians, one cited her before the tribunal upon accusation of debauching married women, when she confessed her sex; they then prosecuted her for having violated the laws, when the matrons, to prevent her ruin, presented themselves before the judges, saying they were not husbands nor children, but enemies, for endeavouring to crush her to whom so many of them owed their lives; upon this, the law pohibiting women to practice midwifery was repealed.

The Lacedemonians bathed new-born children in wine, that they might discover those who were healthy, supposing that the weakly would fall into convulsions, and die when thus bathed. Parents were not allowed to bring up their children, but take them to an appointed place, where, if they were found healthy and strong, they were brought up at the public expence; but, if sickly, detroyed. Among some of the Greeks, parents might disinherit and entirely cast from their protetion their children, provided they went before a magistrate and satisfied him they had cause thereof; and children might dispossess parents of their property, if they proved before a magistrate the parent's incapability of managing it, and their own power of better conducting the same for their mutual advantage.

The passion between the sexes was expressed by various methods, some of which are used by several nations at present; such as inscribing the name of the beloved upon trees, books, &c. Lovers usually decked the doors of their mistresses with flowers and garlands. They also made libations of wine, and sprinkled their doors therewith. When the person's garland was untied, it was taken for a sign that he was in love; and for a woman to make a garland was an indication of her being love. When their love was without success, they had several arts to procure the affections of their beloved. The Thessalian women were famous for their skill in this, as well as other magical practices. They used various means, such as incantations or potions; the operations of the latter were generally violent and dangerous, and commonly deprived such as used them of their reason.

Plutarch and Cornelius Nepos report, that Lucullus, the Roman general, first lost his reason and then his life by one of them. Lucretius, the poet, ended his life the same way; and Caius Caligula (as Suetonius says) was driven into a fit of madness by a philtre given him by his wife

Cæsonia. They used several sorts of herbs, &c. to excite the passion; also insects bred out of putrid matter; lizards, the brains of a calf, the hair upon the extremity of a wolf's tail, with some of his private parts; the bones of the left side of a toad eaten by ants, those of the right side were thought to generate hatred; blood of doves, bones of snakes, bands of wool twisted upon a wheel, which, for their resemblance to the soft ties of love, were very much used upon such occasions, particularly such as had been bound round one who had hanged himself.

Whatever had any relation to funerals or dead bodies was esteemed useful in such cases; sometimes they placed a nest of young swallows in the ground till they were famished; those which died with their mouths shut were thought to be conducive to allay the passion of love; those with their mouths open they supposed would excite love. Some thought the udder of a hyena tied about their left arm a good expedient to win the affections of any woman they looked upon; it was likewise customary to melt wax over a fire, which they thought would tend to mollify and soften the heart of the person he loved as the wax melted, at the same time they repeated the following lines:—

> As this devoted wax melts o'er the fire,
> Let Myndian Delphis melt with soft desire.

Sometimes they burned laurel, repeating as follows:—

> First, Delphid injur'd me, he rais'd my flame,
> And now I burn this bow in Delphid's name;
> As this doth blaze and break away in fume,
> How soon it takes, let Delphid's flesh consume.

If they could get into their possession any thing which belonged to the person beloved, it was esteemed of singular utility. They were particular that love-knots should only consist of three knots, as supposing that number to be more acceptable to the deity.

Love of boys, &c. among the Greeks.—— WHO it was that first introduced the custom of loving boys among the Greeks is uncertain; however, (to omit the infamous amours of Jupiter, Orpheus, Lajus of Thebes, and others,) we find it generally practised by the ancient Grecians, and that not only in private, but by the public allowance and encouragement of their laws; for they thought there could be no means more effectual to excite their youth to noble understanding, nor any greater security to their common-wealths than this passion. This the invaders of their liberty so often experienced, that it became a received maxim in the politics of tyrants, to use all their endeavours to extirpate it out of their dominions; on the contrary, free common-wealths, and all those states that consulted their own honour, seem to have been unanimous in establishing laws to encourage and reward it.

We find it to have been so generally practised and highly esteemed in Crete, that such of their well-born and beautiful youths as never had any lovers incurred the public censure, as persons some way or other faulty in their morals, as if nothing else could hinder, but that some one's affections would be placed upon them; but those that were more happy in being admired, were honoured with the first seats at public exercises, and wore, for a distinguished badge of honour, a sort of garment richly adorned, which they retained, after arriving at man's estate, in memory that they had once been *eminent*, for so the Cretans called the youths who had lovers. One thing was remarkable in this place, that the adopters always took the adopted by force; for, having placed their affections upon any one, they informed his relations thereof, and also what day they intended to take him. If the lover were unworthy to have the boy, they refused to yield him up; but if they thought proper to trust the boy with him, they made a slight opposition to satisfy the law, pursuing him to his residence, when they gave their consent. After this, he carried the boy where he pleased; those who were present at the commencement of the ceremony bearing company. He entertained the youth some time, two months at the farthest, with hunting and other diversions: he then returned him home. At his departure, the law specified that the boy should receive a suit of armour, an ox, and a cup, to which the lover usually added, out of his own bounty, several other presents.

The boy, on his return home, sacrificed the ox to Jupiter, made an entertainment for those that had accompanied him, and gave an account of the usage he had received; for, in case he had been rudely treated, the law allowed him satisfaction. It is further affirmed by Maximus, the Tyrian, that, during all the time of their converse together, nothing unseemly, nothing repugnant to the strictest laws of virtue, passed between them; and however some authors have inclined to have hard thoughts of this custom, yet the testimonies of several others, with the high characters given by the ancients of the old Cretan Constitution, by which this custom was approved, are sufficient to vindicate it from all false imputations. The same is put beyond dispute by what Strabo tells us, that it was not so much the external beauty of the boy as his virtuous disposition, his modesty, and courage, which recommended him.

From the Cretans we pass to the Lacedemonians, several of whose constitutions were derived from Crete. Their love of boys was remarkable all over Greece, and for the whole conduct and excellent consequences of it every where admired. There was no such thing as presents passed between the lovers; no foul arts were used to insinuate themselves into each other's affections; their love was generous, and worthy the Spartan education; it was first instituted from a mutual esteem of each other's virtue, and the same cause which first inspired the flame alone served to nourish and continue it; it was not tainted with so much as a suspicion of immodesty. Agesilaus is said to have refused to kiss the boy he loved, for fear of censure.

If a person attempted any thing with a youth he loved, not consistent with the strictest decorum, the laws adjudged him to disgrace, whereby he was condemned to lose almost all the privileges of a free denizen. The same practice was also common among the females, it being customary for the most virtuous and steady of the illustrious women to acknowledge a passion for a modest and amiable young woman; which is the farther confirmation of the innocence of this custom. Maximus the Tyrian assures us, the Spartans loved their boys no otherwise than a man may be enamoured of a beautiful statue, which he proves from what Plutarch reports, that, though several might admire one boy, yet it occasioned no fears or jealousies among them; but rather was the foundation of a mutual friendship and good understanding between them, while they jointly endeavoured to render the boy, by their united efforts, the most accomplished and respectable of the age; for the very intent and end of this love was, that the object thereof should be induced to follow the path of glory and virtue by conversing with men of probity and talents, whence the adoptor shared the disgrace incurred by the adopted. Plutarch has a story of a Spartan fined by the magistrate because the boy he loved cried out effeminately whilst he was fighting.

The same regard was preserved to man's estate, the youth being directed by his patron, to whom he imparted his concerns, as appears from another relation by Plutarch of Cleomenes, who, before his advancement to the kingdom, was beloved by one Xenares, with whom he ever after maintained a most intimate friendship.

Dr. Clarke, in his *Travels into Russia*, gives us the following account of a marriage ceremony, according to the rites of the Greek church. "We arrived at Akmetchet as Professor Pallas was preparing to celebrate the marriage of his daughter, according to the rites of the Greek church, with Baron Wimfeldt, an Hungarian general in the Russian service. The wedding took place on the following day, Saturday, Aug. 9, 1800, after a superb dinner. At the doors they were met by the priest. The general was asked, if he was already related to the lady by any tie of blood; on his answering in the negative, the same question was again put to the intended bride, and was answered in the same way. They were asked then, whether the engagement they were about to form was voluntary on their part; and, having answered in the affirmative, were permitted to enter a few paces from the church. A bible and crucifix were then placed before them, and large lighted wax tapers, decorated with ribbons, put in their hands; after certain prayers had been read, and the ring put upon the bride's finger, the floor was covered by a piece of scarlet satin, and a table was placed before them with the communion vessels. The priest, having tied their hands together with bands of the same coloured satin, and placed a chaplet of flowers upon their heads, administered the sacrament; and afterwards led them, thus bound together, three times round the communion-table, followed by the bride's father and the bride-maid. During this ceremony the choristers chanted a hymn; and, after it was concluded, a scene of general kissing took place among all present, and the parties returned to the house of the bride's father; here tea and other refreshments were served to all who came to congratulate the married couple.

"We remained a month at Akmetchet, before my health was again established; during this time I had an opportunity of seeing so remarkable a ceremony at a Jew's wedding, that a short account of it cannot be unentertaining.

"For two or three days prior to the wedding, all the neighbours and friends of the betrothed couple assembled together, to testify their joy by the most tumultuous rioting, dancing, and feasting. On the day of marriage the girl, accompanied by the priest and her relations, was led blindfolded to the river Salgir, which flowed at the botton of a small valley in front of Professor Pallas's house. Here she was undressed by women who were stark naked, and, destitute of any other covering except the handkerchief by which her eyes were concealed, was plunged three times in the river. After this, being again dressed, she was led, blindfolded as before, to the house of her parents, accompanied by all her friends, who were singing, dancing, and performing music before her. In the evening her intended husband was brought to her; but, as long as the feast continued, she remained with her eyes bound."

In the *Irish Philosophical Transactions* for 1789, we have a description of the island of Metellis, by the Earl of Charlemont, in which he speaks with rapture of its beauties. He then describes a most remarkable custom of the women's usurping that sovereignty which in other countries is exercised as a right by men. Contrary to the usage of all other countries, here the eldest daughter inherits the family estates; and the sons, like as daughters are every where else, are portioned off with small dowers, or, what is worse, turned out pennyless to seek their fortune. If a man have two daughters, the eldest is entitled to all her mother's possessions, which are by far the greater part of the family estate, for the mother, keeping up her prerogative, never parts with her power over any part she may have brought into the family, until there is a necessity for it by the marriage of her eldest daughter, and the father also is compelled to add whatever he can spare, even to their almost ruin.

The second daughter inherits nothing, and is doomed to perpetual celibacy; she is styled a *calogria*, the proper signification of which is a nun or religious person, and is in effect a menial servant to her sister, being employed by her in any office she may think fit to impose, frequently serving her as a waiting-maid, cook, and often in employments more degrading. She wears a habit peculiar to her situation, which she can never change; it consists of a sort of monastic dress, coarse, and of a dark brown. One, advantage, however, she enjoys over her sister, that, whereas the elder, before marriage, is never allowed to go abroad, or to see any man, her nearest relations only excepted, the *calogria*, except when employed in domestic business, is in this respect at perfect liberty.

But when the sister is married, the situation of the poor *calogria* is desperate indeed, and is rendered still more humiliating by comparing her condition with that of her happy sister. The married sister enjoys every sort of liberty; the whole family fortune is hers, and she spends it as she pleases; her husband is her obsequious servant, her ather and mother are dependent upon her; she dresses in the most magnificent manner after the fashion of the island, covered all over with pearls, diamonds, and pieces of gold, which are most commonly sequins; thus, continually carrying about her the marks of affluence and prosperity, while the wretched *calogria* follows her as a servant, arrayed in simple homespun brown, without the most distant hope of ever altering her condition.

Such a disparity may seem intolerable, but what will not custom reconcile? Neither are the misfortunes of the family yet at an end; the father and the mother by their industry and frugality endeavour to accumulate and collect yet a little substance, which, if they have a third daughter, must also be parted with to her, the fourth daughter being *calogria* to the third; and so on through all the daughters alternately.

Whenever a daughter is marriageable, she can by custom compel her father to procure her a husband, which the mother never fails to teaze him to, notwithstanding the ruinous effects of it on both of them. From whence it happens that nothing is more common than for the father and mother to be reduced to indigence, whilst their married daughter is surrounded with affluence, parading the streets in all the luxury of wealth, followed by their parents, sisters, &c. as menial servants.

The sons, as soon as they are of age to gain a livelihood, are turned out of the family, sometimes with a small present or portion, but more frequently without any thing to support them; and thus turned adrift they endeavour to support themselves by their labour; or, what is more common, go on board a fishing smack, or some trading vessel, where they continue till they have saved a little money, and then return home to marry and be henpecked. Some few there are who, taking advantage of the Turkish law, marry a *culogria*, and retain in their own hands their property and authority. But these are accounted men of a singular and even criminal disposition, and are hated and despised as conformists to Turkish manners, and deserters of their native customs; so that we may suppose the number is comparatively small who have the boldness to desert the manners of their native country, and adopt those of the Turks, who are their detested masters, and thereby have the contempt, hatred, and derision, of their fellow-citizens and countrymen.

In Corea, another of the Greek islands, the marriage ceremony is as follows:—On the day of marriage, the bridegroom mounts his steed, and, attended by his friends, rides about the town, making several circuits, till he stops at the door of the bride, upon which her relations come out and conduct her to his house, when the marriage is consummated without any further ceremony. A man is allowed by the Corean law to have several wives, provided he only keeps one at home. The grandees, indeed, sometimes keep two or three at home; but only one acts as supreme mistress. Upon the whole, it does not appear that they have any tender attachment to their wives, as they are treated little better than slaves.

Among the Coreans, if a woman kill her husband, she is put into the ground, leaving only her head out, by the side of the highway, and every passenger, by law, must take a chop at her head with an axe which is laid by for the purpose; none but those of noble blood being excused from striking the delinquent. A man is allowed to kill his wife if he detect her in adultery; if he deliver her to the magistrate, she may choose her own death, which they generally execute by cutting their own throats. Some travellers have asserted that husbands, especially those of noble extraction, suffer death for adultery.

When an unmarried man is detected in *crim. con.* with a married woman, they strip him to the waist, leaving him only a pair of drawers on; his face is smeared with lime, an arrow is pierced through both his ears, and a kettle tied upon his back, which is beat upon as the offender walks through the streets: he then receives the bastinado.

In the islands of Socotora the inhabitants have many strange and singular customs. They allow of polygamy, and divorce their wives at pleasure, either for life or a certain time. A man may be the reputed father of children without having any of his own, or even having a wife to support, which is thus; if a man, during a woman's pregnancy to him, prevail upon her to allow of his giving the child away as soon as it sees the light, he kindles a fire at the door of his hut, and then makes proclamation that he will give away the infant of which his wife is with child, as soon as it is born. Upon the birth of the infant, he sends it to some man whom he has chosen to be its adopted parent, where it meets with all those attentions denied by its natural father. A nurse is provided, and every care taken of the infant.

These children are called the sons or daughters of *smoke*; and it frequently happens that a good-natured man, who has no children of his own, will have a dozen in this manner imposed upon him. This is certainly one of the most extraordinary circumstances to be met with in history; nor can it be accounted for either on political or natural principles, as a father, who exposes his own child, will perhaps adopt the children of others.

GERMANY, SWEDEN, &c.

FORMERLY among the Northen nations in general, the females were treated with a degree of respect and confidence unknown among the Southern states, and, so high was their opinion of the judgment and discretion of their women, that they were very frequently consulted upon state affairs.—The ancient Germans carried their respect for the fair sex so far, that the fine for baring the arm of a free woman against her wish was fifteen shillings, as much as for cutting off the finger of a man; and if a man had the temerity to touch her bosom, he was fined forty shillings, as much as for cutting off the nose or three fingers of a warrior. A kiss snatched from a female was punished with exile; if with her consent, but without the knowledge of her husband or brother, he was fined three marks of silver.

But if they were thus solicitous to guard their females from insult, and any improper or licentious liberty, they were still more severe towards them if they violated their marriage vow, and they punished the crime of adultery in the following manner:—The guilty wife (her hair, as a mark of ignominy, being cut off) was expelled from the dwelling of the man she had injured, and in the presence of her husband she was stripped quite naked; she was then pursued through the town by her revengeful husband, beating her all the way with the most unrelenting cruelty, and then turned adrift without any notice being taken of her by either her friends or relations.

The following is a description of a marriage procession at Holstein, by Sir John Carr. "In the morning, as the horses were putting to, a singular procession passed us; a young woman in gala, whose hair was stiffened to the consistence of stucco with pomatum and powder, on which was raised a high cap of lace, decorated with a profusion of artificial flowers, and a large nosegay of natural and artificial flowers in her bosom, and a book in her hand, and turning in her toes most abominably, passed in the most stately manner up the street, preceded by three girls in mob caps, decorated with little bits of gold and silver lace, dressed in red jackets, each with a book in her hand, and followed by two old women with books also. The fair heroine of this singular group moved to me as she passed. She was proceeding to the church, where the bridegroom was counting the lingering moments of her absence. Old and young peeped out of the doors and windows as the cavalcade passed."

Among the *Lithuanians*, a woman is not looked upon as marriageable till she is twenty-four years of age. She must also have made with her own hands a quantity of clothes, which at the time of her espousal she is to distribute among the guests which the bridegroom shall bring to the wedding; she must likewise have served her mother in all domestic affairs for a certain time.

Those employed to negociate a match always inquire very strictly into the manners and behaviour of the party treated for. Some of the girls are so reserved, that they will draw a knife at a man who only offers to kiss them.

SWEDEN.—Among the Swedes marriages are generally governed entirely by the will of the parents, and founded so much upon interest, that the inclination of the parties is very little regarded, nor the relations much troubled with the extravagancies of lovers. A stolen match is hardly ever heard of in an age, nor can the church give licence to marry without the publication of the banns. Persons of quality of either sex commonly remain single till they are thirty, and sometimes longer, as the fortune on both sides is in the hands of the parents, which they retain till death; the young couple have therefore no means of support till that period, unless they obtain some office or employment. The women in general are more distinguished for their chastity before marriage than for their fidelity after. They are no where made greater drudges than here; the meaner sort being, besides the ordinary office of the sex, put to plough and thrash, to row in boats, and bear burdens in building of houses, and other occasions. Domestic quarrels seldom happen, and, when they do, are very seldom made public, the husbands being apt to keep the authority in their own hands, as the wives by inclination are mostly obedient.

Divorces and other separations between married persons are very rare, and what happen are chiefly among the lower order: the innocent party only is allowed to marry again.—Cousin-germans are not permitted to marry without the king's dispensation, which is generally granted. In their wedding entertainments they ever affect pomp and superfluity, so much beyond their ability, that, often by their excess at one entertainment, they are involved in difficulties for several years.

The marriage customs of the inhabitants of Möuchgut, in Rugen Island, are rather of a singular nature, and tend much to shew the manners and disposition of the inhabitants. Neither man nor woman ever thinks of matrimony till they are in possession of a kath or cottage; and as soon as the parties are agreed, the consent of their ground landlord is requested. In the afternoon of the wedding day, the relations and friends of the bridegroom repair to his house, and *vice versa* with the bride, each inviting their friends separately. The two parties proceed towards the church-yard, where they unite; the bridegroom then salutes his intended by pressing her hand. If the bride belong to another village, she takes leave of her relations with tears, as if she were never more to behold them. After the ceremony in the church is over, both sexes separate, and the females retire to the warm beer-house, where one of them presents the bride with some warm beer, and desires her in a verse to drink beer with all her friends, and make herself happy till they meet in Heaven.

The warm beer, plentifully studded with large raisins, is circulated briskly till towards evening, when the discharge of a pistol summons them to the bridegroom's dwelling, where an immense dish of rice constitutes the first course, which is succeeded by a variety of others; during which time, the cup bearer is actively employed. The dress of the bride is little more ornamental than usual, excepting a wreath she wears on her head, above which is a kind of a crown, made of box twigs, having the leaves gilt or silvered; her hair is dressed for the purpose, stiffened and glossed with the white of eggs.—The bridegroom is distinguished by a large white handkerchief, a present from the bride, the corners of which hang down low in the front. Should he, however, have obtained *jus primæ noctis* before marriage, the ends of the handkerchief must be carefully concealed.

The POLES, in their marriage contracts, do not inquire what a girl's portion is, but how many relations she has; it being the custom of that country for all the relations to give the bride something at her wedding; nor is it looked upon as discreditable among them for the females to propose a match, which is always done through the medium of relations.

Those men and women, who are godfathers and godmothers to the same children, are looked upon as cousins to each other, and cannot marry together without first obtaining a dispensation.

RUSSIA.

The Russian women are fair, comely, strong, and well shaped, obedient to their lordly husbands, and patient under discipline; they are even said to be fond of correction, which they consider as an infallible mark of their husband's conjugal affection, and they pout and pine as if they thought themselves treated with disregard and contempt. Of this neglect, however, they have very little cause to complain, the Russian husband being generally disposed both by nature and inebriation to exercise his arbitrary power. Some writers say that on the wedding day the bride presents the bridegroom with a whip of her own making, in token of submission, and with this he fails not to show his authority.

The nuptials ceremonies of the Russians are very singular. When the parents have agreed upon the match, (though the parties perhaps have never seen each other,) the bride is critically examined by a number of women, in order to discover if she has any bodily defect, and, if any, to remedy it if possible. The bride on her wedding-day is crowned with a garland of wormwood, implying the bitterness of the married state. When the priest has tied the nuptials knot at the altar, the clerk or sexton sprinkles on her head a handful of hops, wishing she may be as fruitful as that plant. She is muffled up and led home by a certain number of old women, the priest carrying the cross before, while one of his subalterns, clad in a rough goat skin, prays all the way that she may have as many children as there are hairs on his garment. The new-married couple, being seated at table, are presented with bread and salt, whilst a chorus of boys and girls sing the epithalamium, which is always grossly obscene.

This ceremony being performed, the bride and bridegroom are conducted to their own chamber by an old woman, who exhorts the bride to be obedient to her husband, and retires. The bridegroom then desires the bride to pull off one of his buskins, giving her to understand that one of them contains a whip, and the other a jewel or a purse of money. She takes her choice; if she find the purse, she interprets it as a good omen; but, if she find the whip, it is looked upon as an unhappy presage, and she immediately receives a lash as a specimen of what she is to expect. After they have remained two hours together, they are visited by a deputation of old women, who come to search for the signs of her virginity; if these be apparent, the young lady ties up her hair, which before her consummation hung in loose tresses over her shoulders, and visits her mother, of whom she demands her marriage portion.

It is generally agreed that the Muscovite husbands are barbarous, even to a proverb; they not only administer severe correction to their wives, but sometimes even torture them to death, without being subject to any punishment for the murder. The canon law of Muscovy forbids the conjugal intercourse on Mondays, Wednesdays, and Fridays, and whoever transgresses this law must bathe himself before he enters the church porch. He that marries a second wife, the first being alive, is not admitted farther into the church than the door; but if he marry a third, he is excommunicated; so that, though they tolerate bigamy, it is accounted infamous.

If a woman be barren, the husband generally persuades her to retire into a convent; if fair means will not succeed, he is at liberty to whip her into condescension. When the Czar or Emperor has a mind to a wife, the most beautiful maidens of the country are presented to him for his choice.

The education of the Czarowitz, or Prince Royal, is entrusted to the care of a few persons, who scrupulously seclude his person from the eyes of the vulgar, until he has attained the fifteenth year of his age; he is then publicly exposed in the market-place, that the people, by viewing him attentively, may remember his person, in order to ascertain his identity; for they have more than once been deceived by impostors.

Such is the slavery by which the Muscovites of both sexes are kept by their parents, patrons, and emperor, that they are not allowed to dispute any match that is provided for them by those directors, however disagreeable or odious it may be. Officers of the highest rank in the army, both natives and foreigners, have been wedded with wives by the sovereigns in this arbitrary manner. A great general, some time since deceased, who was a native of Britain, having been pressed by the late Czarina to wed one of her ladies, saved himself from a very disagreeable match by pretending that, from the unsoundness of his constitution, the lady would be irreparably injured by his compliance.

Sir John Carr gives the following account of the penance which was imposed on an adultress.

"In one of the churches I saw a woman doing penance for the following crime: – she had not long been married before she polluted the bed of her husband, whom she used to keep in an almost constant state of inebriation. One day, when she was indulging with one of her gallants, the husband, whom she supposed stupified with drink, unexpectedly appeared sober, and, stung with jealousy, he stabbed his rival to the heart. The husband was knouted, and sent to Siberia; the wife was ordered by the priest to prostrate herself six hundred times a day for two years before the virgin."

If a Russian woman should kill her husband while he is chastising her, which they sometimes do from the severities they receive, she is buried in the ground with her head only uncovered, and in this state she is left to perish; sometimes they remain several days before death relieves them. The females in general are treated with great disrespect, and the only chance they have of being comfortable in the married state, is when their parents bind the husband by agreement before marriage not to use any unnecessary correction. Many of the married females lead very dissolute lives, frequently accompanying their husbands in their bacchanalian debaucheries.

The amatory customs of the KAMSCHATDALES are very singular. When a man fixes his affections upon a female, he binds himself to the service of the parents for a limited time, at the expiration of which he either obtains their consent to marry her, or a requital for his services upon dismission. If he obtain the consent of the father, they proceed to the nuptial ceremonies, which consist in the bridegroom stripping the bride of her clothes, which are purposely bound so fast with straps, girdles, and other ligaments, as to render it a very difficult task. The bride is assisted against his efforts by the interposition of several women, notwithstanding which he persists in his purpose till her exclamations bring them all upon him, and he is used so roughly that he exhibits several marks of their indignation. At length the bride, moved with pity for his situation, and the women relaxing their fury, the man is called back with a plaintive tone by the bride, who confesses his conquest over her. Here ends the ceremony; and the happy pair, the ensuing day, proceed to the habitation of the husband. In the course of a week they pay a visit to the parents of the bride, the relations of both parties are assembled, and the marriage is celebrated with great festivity. Some men marry three wives, who live together in an amicable manner, and are seldom or never jealous. When the women go abroad they veil their faces, and, if they meet a man, and cannot get out of the way, they turn their back to him till he has passed by. Though the very attempt to procure abortion is esteemed a capital crime in a woman, yet, when twins are born, one of the innocents must be destroyed. Infants, as soon as they can stand, are left to themselves by the mother, suffering them to roll on the ground. The children go nearly naked, and begin to walk at a time when a child in Europe would scarcely stand; soon after they begin to run about in the snow.

Among the ZAPOROG COSSACKS, it is not the custom to live with women as is usual among other people; but each form a separate community, living entirely independent of each other. The women live in villages by themselves, each village being governed by an Attaman, and were forbidden, upon pain of death, to come to the Setch, or residence of the men. Each Zaporog had a right to go to the women when, and select those, he chose. When a woman was pregnant, no person gave himself any trouble to ascertain who was the father of the child, as it belonged to the nation at large. If it were a boy, he was brought into the Setch at the age of four years, and was educated these; but a girl was continued with the mother, and, as soon as of age, obliged to submit to the embraces of any free Zaporog who might take a fancy to cohabit with her. Four women always live in the same hut together. If a man fell in love with a girl, he was allowed to marry her; but he lost all right to share in the produce of the chase, and was obliged to till the land, and pay a certain tribute, which was divided amongst the Zaporogs of the Setch who stiled themselves free and noble.— It is a singular fact, that marriage *was* greatly respected by this savage nation, and that, from the moment a marriage was concluded, no Zaporog dared invade the conjugal rites of his neighbour, an ignominious death being the punishment for adultery.

The OSTIACS of Siberia, who still adhere to paganism, take as many wives as they can afford to keep. Among them it is legal to marry their brother's widow, their step-mother, step-daughter, and other relations. They are fond of marrying sisters of other families, and believe that marrying their wife's sister brings good luck; and by doing this they only pay their father half the price, or kalym, paid for the first. But they hold it sinful to marry relations of the same name; yet they attend only to the male line. If a woman have married into another family and borne a daughter, the brother of the mother, or his children, marry that daughter. In short, all marriages are legal, if only the father of the couple be of different families.

Among the KOREKI, they generally marry in their own family; father and daughter, mother and son, being the only prohibition for consanguinity. The wandering Korcki are very jealous, frequently putting their wives to death upon very slight suspicions; when detected in adultery, both the man and the woman are inevitably put to death. Therefore, their women seldom bestow any pains in ornamenting themselves. The settled Koreki are quite the reverse; they always, when one man visits another, present their wife or daughter for him to lie with. The marriage ceremony of both is as follows:—when a man has a fancy to any particular female, he goes to reside with her parents, and at the end of a certain period they either let him have their daughter, or pay for his services during that period; in the former case, he goes to the tent of the bride, and endeavours to strip her naked, in which he is stoutly opposed by several women, who tear his hair and scratch his face; he then seems as if he would retreat, but is called back by the relenting bride, and, the attendants retiring, the marriage is consummated.

With the SAMOIEDES, however, the custom is somewhat different, who, when he wants a wife, looks for her in some other family than his own. Beauty is not an object; they choose one equal to themselves in rank and property. Having appointed a person from among his own friends to transact the business, the negociator waits upon the father of the young woman, and inquires whether the young man can have her. If the father accept the proposal, the negociator settles the kalym, or price to be paid, which generally consists of a variety of clothes, household necessaries, rein deer, and other matters purchased from the Russians. As soon as the youth has paid the kalym, it is settled when the bride's portion is to be paid, and when she shall be ready to give her hand. On the day appointed, the bridegroom attends with a number of women to fetch the bride; they are then married.— In case of divorce, the kalym is returned. Should the woman die soon after the marriage, the widower claims a return to the kalym, if respect for the deceased do not prevent the return.

The ALEUTIANS take one, two, or three wives, as they have the means of supporting them. They have no nuptial ceremonies. The bridegroom commonly treats with the parents for the bride, and promises what he thinks he can afford, either in clothes, baidars, or what are termed Kalga, which is prisoners made in other islands, or destitute orphans, who are consigned over to a rich Aleutian to labour for their bare subsistence, and may be transferred to another on the same conditions. When the parties are agreed, the bridegroom begins to visit the bride, when he spends whole days with her in the character of a lover. If they have any regard for each other, the bridegroom either takes her to his dwelling or repairs for a continuance to hers; and, if they continue to live in harmony, the bride's father makes presents to his son-in-law; on the contrary, should the man not be satisfied with his wife, he may send her to her father again, but has no right to demand his own presents back again; but, should the woman refuse to stay with him, in that case he may demand back all that he gave for her. No man is allowed to sell his wife without her consent; but he can resign her over to another either for a term of years or for a continuance, which is not unfrequent. The Russian hunters in particular make use of this privilege, and take Aleutian women or girls for a time, for which they give a trifling compensation. It never happens that a wife grants her favours without the consent of her husband; for in this barter of their persons they are not influenced by love, but merely the desire of gain; nor was this custom so frequent before the arrival of the Russians, neither is it practiced by any but those whose thirst of gain has stifled their natural sense of shame; there are, however, many who would not for any emolument whatever allow of so disgraceful a practice. It is said, that formerly gain was not the motive, but a sort of compassion and cordial attachment to an individual upon his return after a long absence. Hence it is that the husband, who can never claim the children with any certainty as his own, has not an equally unlimited power over them with the mother; nay, he has less authority over them than their uncles by the mother's side. The children of one father by different mothers are not considered as brothers and sisters, but are permitted to intermarry. The distribution of the father's property at his decease is regulated by his relations, who usually leave the larger part for his widows and children, and take the rest themselves. If the wife have an affection for the deceased, she cuts the hair off the crown of her head, and keeps the body for some time in the hut before it is interred, frequently several weeks. A mother too will often keep the body of a dead child till she has another, which is sometimes kept twelve months on that account.

LAPLAND, GREENLAND, ICELAND.

THE Lapland marriage customs are very remarkable and ludicrous. When a young man has made choice of a female, he employs some friends as mediators with the girl's parents.—The negociators, being supplied with several bottles of brandy, proceed therewith to the hut of the girl's father, accompanied by the suitor, but he is not allowed to enter until the liquor is drunk, over which they discuss the proposal. The lover is then called in, and entertained with such fare as the hut affords, but without seeing his mistress, who, on this occasion, is obliged to retire. When he has obtained permission to pay his addresses to the girl in person, he goes home, dresses himself in his best attire, and returns to the hut; when his mistress makes her appearance, he salutes her with a kiss, and presents her with the tongue of a rein-deer, a piece of beaver's flesh, or some kind of provision. The girl at first declines the offer, it being in the presence of her relations, but she makes a sign for him to follow her out, and she there accepts of his presents. He then requests permission to sleep with her in the hut, which is obtained if she keep the presents, otherwise she throws them with disdain on the ground, which is a rejection of his addresses.

When the lovers have agreed, he is allowed to visit his mistress as often as he pleases, but each time he must bring a bottle of brandy, a perquisite so agreeable to the girl's father, that for the sake of it he will often postpone the celebration of the nuptials for a year or two. At length the ceremony is performed at the nearest church, but even after this the bridegroom must serve his father-in-law a whole year; at the expiration of which time he retired to his own habitation with his wife, and receives presents from his friends and relatives. From this time he sequesters his wife from the company of all strangers, especially of the male sex, and watches over her conduct with the most jealous vigilance.

When a lover goes to pay a visit to his mistress, during his journey through the fenny moors he usually diverts himself with a song, which he addresses to his rein-deer. A translation of one of these from the original, which Professor Scheffer obtained from Olaus Matthias, a native of Lapland, we shall present for the entertainment of our readers.

The circumstances that successively present themselves to him during his journey are naturally interwoven. The anxiety of absence, the gloominess of the roads, and his resolution of frequenting them, as those only can carry him to the object of his wishes; the dissatisfaction he expresses even at the great rapidity with which he travels, and joyful surprise at the unexpected sight of his mistress as she is bathing, are all beautifully described in the following composition:—

A Laplander's Song to his Rein-Deer.

HASTE, my rein-deer, and let us nimbly go
  Our am'rous journey thro' this dreary waste;
Haste, my rein-deer, still, still thou art too slow,
  Impetuous love demands the lightning's haste.

Around us far the rushy moors are spread;
  Soon will the sun withdraw its cheerful ray;
Darkling and tir'd we shall the marshes tread,
  No lay unstrung to cheat the tedious way.

The wat'ry length of these unjoyous moors
  Does all the flow'ry meadow's pride excel;

Through these I fly to her my soul adores;
  Ye flow'ry meadows, empty pride, farewell.

Each moment from the charmer I'm confin'd,
  My breast is tortur'd with impatient fires;
Fly, my rein-deer, fly swifter than the wind;
  Thy tardy feet wing with my swift desires.

Our pleasing toil will then be soon o'erpaid,
  And thou, in wonder lost, shalt view my fair;
Admire each feature of the lovely maid,
  Her artless charms, her bloom, her sprightly air.

But, lo! with graceful motion there she swims,
  Gently removing each ambitious wave;
The crowding waves transported clasp her limbs!
  When, when, oh! when shall I such freedom have?

In vain, ye envious streams, so fast ye flow,
  To hide her from a lover's ardent gaze;
From ev'ry touch you more transparent grow,
  And all reveal'd the beauteous wanton plays.

To this we add a Lapland love-song by the same author, and procured by the above-mentioned Professor.

A Lapland Love-song.

Source of my daily thoughts and nightly dreams,
  Whose captivating beauties I adore;
Oh may the radiant sun's refulgent beams
  Shine on the charms of lovely *Orra Moor!*

I'd climb the summit of the lofty pine,
  Could I my *Orra Moor* at distance view;
No labour, danger, care, would I decline,
  To see my charmer, and to find her true.

Could she be wafted to terrestrial bow'rs,
  And there in pleasant shades induc'd to stay,
Or range enamell'd fields of sweetest flow'rs,
  Charm'd by the birds that warbled on each spray,

Enrag'd, I would those pretty birds destroy,
  Pluck up the flow'rs that beautify the field,
Cut down the bow'rs that rob me of my joy,
  And from my view my beauteous *Orra* shield!

Oh! that I could but soar into the sky,
  And wing my passage thro' th' ambient air,
Swift as the feather'd race could I but fly,
  I'd soon be with my captivating fair.

But vain, alas! my wishes are but vain;
  No stork, no raven, will a pinion lend;
Fatal to feel unmitigated pain,
  With scarce a hope my passion to befriend.

So long my bliss can *Orra Moor* delay?
  Reflect the summer's sun now brightly gleams!
Short are our summers, haste, then haste away,
  And with my love enjoy his glad'ning beams.

Alas! unkindly you delay the time,
  Our short-liv'd summer wears away a pace;
You've tortur'd me, and trifle with your prime,
  Till frowning winter shows his rugged face.

Still, still my lovely charmer I'll pursue,
And scorn all danger to reveal my pains;
For what can't love, all-pow'rful love subdue?
He laughs at tempests and despises chains.

Love, mighty victor, triumphs o'er mankind,
Brings ev'ry thought beneath his own controul;
Enslaves the heart, puts fetters on the mind,
And captivates the haughty human soul.

But hark! stern reason whispers in my ear,
"Friend, you are wrong, thus to pour oil on fire
Rashly to follow what we ought to fear,
And rush into a whirlwind of desire.

A thousand things advise you to desist,
A thousand dread examples bid you view
The fate of those whom love's delusive mist
Hath slily blinded, sadly to undo."

Reason, avaunt! to passion I submit,
And will not hear thy disempassion'd tone;
Others thy thousand counsellors may fit,
But I'll attend the voice of love alone!

As soon as a child is born, it is washed all over with snow or cold water, except its head, which must not be touched with water until after it is baptized; for the performing of which ceremony, the mother, after her recovery, is frequently obliged to traverse immense forests and waters, covered with snow, before she comes to a priest or church.

The Laplanders are fond of having a numerous family, but very seldom have more than seven or eight children.

GREENLAND.—The marriage ceremonies in Greenland are very similar to those in Lapland. When a young Greenlander feels affection for a maiden, he proposes it to the parents on both sides; and, after he has obtained their consent, he gets two or more women to fetch the bride; sometimes he fetches her himself, which must be done by force; for, though she ever so much approve of the match, the custom of the country does not allow of any appearance thereof. When she is brought to the bridegroom's house, she sits retired in a corner, with her hair dishevelled and covering her face, the bridegroom using all the rhetoric he is master of to persuade her to comply with his ardent wishes; to which she at length consents, and the wedding is then over.

So much repugnance have some of their young women to matrimony, that, when their father proposes a match to them, they frequently run into the woods, or cut off their hair; after the latter, they are in no danger of addresses from any other man, it being considered the greatest disgrace that can possibly happen to a female.

Their reluctance proceeds from the hardships they labour under in the wedded state. Not so with the married women who have grown-up sons, their situations being comparatively enviable; the sons supporting the mother, either in their own house or, if the father be dead, in his house, where the mother only is mistress, even over the wives of her sons.

The Greenlanders seldom marry a near relation, or, indeed, any person bred up with them; but there are some instances of a man marrying two sisters, or a mother and daughter. Being thought a reproach not to have a son, it sometimes leads men into polygamy, though it is not very general, scarcely one in twenty having more than one wife. If a woman do not breed, she is sometimes put away, and this with little more ceremony on the part of the man than a sour look, and then packing up the clothes of the woman: when this happens, the woman returns to her friends, and conducts herself with the greatest circumspection, in order to bring an odium upon him.—Where a wife cannot agree with other women in the house, she will elope, especially if she have no sons; as sons are the pride of a Greenlander's heart, his greatest treasure, and the best security he has for his possessions.

The ICELANDERS, at their weddings, are adorned in a very singular manner. The bride wears, close to the face, round her head dress, a crown of silver gilt. She has two chains round her neck, one hangs down low, and the other rests on her shoulders. Besides these, she wears a smaller chain, from whence hangs a little heart, into which they put some kind of perfume. Upon this occasion, all Icelandic women wear such a dress, the only difference consisting in the quality of the cloth and ornaments, some being made of gold and silver, others of brass, &c. Unmarried women wear a different head-dress to the married.

TURKEY AND DALMATIA.

A DESCRIPTION of the Turkish Seraglio being intimately connected with the marriage ceremonies of the Turkish Empire, we give the following from a very intelligent and observing writer.

The word *Seraglio* is used by way of eminence to distinguish the palace of the Grand

Signior at Constantinople, where he keeps his court, and in which his concubines are lodged, and youth are trained up to qualify them to fill the highest offices at court. It is a triangle about three Italian miles round, wholly within the city, at the end of the promontory Chrysorecas, now called the Seraglio Point. The buildings run back to the top of the hill, and from thence there are gardens which reach to the edge of the sea. It is enclosed with a very high and strong wall, upon which there are several watch-towers; it has many gates, some of which open towards the sea side, and others into the city, but the chief gate is one of the latter, which is constantly guarded by a company of capochees, or porters; in the night it is very strongly guarded towards the sea. The outward appearance is not very beautiful, its architecture being irregular, consisting of several separate edifices in the form of pavilions and domes.

The ladies of the Seraglio are a collection of beautiful young women, chiefly sent as presents from the provinces of the Greek islands, most of them being children of Christian parents.— The brave Prince Heraclius abolished the infamous tribute of children of both sexes, which

Georgia formerly paid to the Porte yearly. The number of women in the harem depends on the taste of the reigning Sultan; Selim had two thousand, Achmet had but three hundred, and the late Sultan had nearly sixteen hundred.

On their admission they are committed to the care of old ladies, taught sewing and embroidery, music, dancing, and other accomplishments, and furnished with the richest clothes and ornaments. They all sleep in different beds, and between every fifth there is a preceptress. Their chief governess is called Katon Kiaga, or governess of the noble young ladies. There is not one servant among them, for they are obliged to wait on one another by rotation; the last that is entered serves the one that preceded herself. These ladies are never suffered to go abroad, except when the Grand Signior removes from one place to another, when a troop of black eunuchs conveys them to the boats, which are enclosed with lattices and linen curtains; and when they travel by land, are put into close chariots, and signals are made at certain distances to give notice that none approach the roads through which they pass. The boats of the harem, which carry the Signior's wives, are manned with twenty-four rowers, and have white covered tilts, shut alternately by venetian blinds. Among the Sultan's attendants are a number of mutes, who act and converse by signs with great quickness; also some dwarfs, who are exhibited for the diversion of his majesty.

When he permits the women to walk in the garden of the Seraglio, all the people are ordered to retire, and on every side there is placed a guard of black eunuchs, with sabres drawn in their hands, while others go round in order to see that no person is near who is not belonging to the Seraglio. Should any one be found in the garden, even though it be through ignorance or inadvertence, he is undoubtedly killed, and his head brought and laid at the feet of the Grand Signior, who gives a great reward to the guard which brought it. Sometimes the Grand Signior goes into the gardens to amuse himself while the women are there; and it is then and there that they use their utmost efforts to please and captivate his majesty, by dancing, singing, seducing gestures, and amorous blandishments, by which they endeavour to ensnare the heart of the monarch. It is not permitted to take a virgin to his bed, except during the solemn festivals, or on occasion of some extraordinary rejoicings, or the arrival of some good news. Upon such occasions, if the Sultan choose a new partner to his bed, he enters into the apartments of the women, who are ranged in files by the governess, to whom he speaks and intimates which he likes best.

The ceremony of throwing the handkerchief, as related of the Sultan, to the girl he likes best, is an idle tale without any foundation. As soon as the Grand Signior has chosen the girl that he has destined to be his companion for the night, all the others follow her to the bath, washing and perfuming her; she is then dressed superbly, and conducted to the Sultan's chamber with singing, dancing, and rejoicing, who is generally on such an occasion already in bed. Scarcely has the newly elected favourite reached the chamber of her lord, introduced by the grand eunuch, who is upon guard, than she kneels down, and, when the Sultan calls, she creeps into bed to him at the foot of the bed, unless the Sultan orders her by special grace to approach by the side. After a certain time, upon a signal given by the Signior, the governess of the girls, with all her suite, enters the apartment, and conducts her back with the same ceremony as before, to the woman's apartment. Should she fortunately prove pregnant, and be delivered of a boy, she is called *Asaki Sultaness*, that is to say, Sultaness-mother; for the first son she has the honour of being crowned, and has the liberty of forming a court. She has also an appointed guard of eunuchs for her particular service. None of the other ladies, though delivered of boys, are either crowned or maintained with such costly distinction as the first; however, they have their service apart, and have handsome appointments.

At the death of the Sultan, the mothers of the male children are shut up in the old Seraglio, from whence they are never allowed to come out any more, unless one of their sons ascend the throne. Baron de Tott informs us, that the female slave who chances to be mother of the Sultan, and lives long enough to see her son mount the throne, is the only woman who at that period alone is called Sultana-mother; she is till then shut up in the interior of her prison with her son. The title of *Bache-kadun*, principal woman, is the highest dignity of the Grand Signior's harem; and she has a larger allowance than those who have the title of second, third, or fourth, which are the four free women allowed by the Koran. Lady Wortley Montague says, that, at the time she visited Turkey, (1717,) the widow of the late Sultan was obliged by the reigning Sultan to quit the Seraglio, and choose a husband from among those who were her subjects. She used every argument and intreaty to avoid the disgrace, as it is looked upon; but nothing could prevail with the sovereign to change his determination, and she actually fixed upon a man upwards of fourscore years of age, though she was little more than twenty herself.

Dr. Clarke relates, that, in 1808, the gardener of the Grand Signior was a German, and that, while the secretary to the Swedish mission was in conversation with him, it was announced that the Sultan-mother and four Sultanas were about to take the air in the gardens—They instantly closed the shutters, and locked the doors of the lodge. Through two gimblet holes bored on purpose, they beheld the features of the Sultanas, one of whom was very fair, and all possessed extraordinary beauty. Their dresses were rich beyond all description. Long spangled robes open in front, with pantaloons embroidered with gold and silver, and studded with a profusion of pearls and diamonds, displayed their persons to the greatest advantage. Their hair hung in loose tresses, powdered carelessly with clusters of jewels; a little on one side of the head they wore small diadems, and their faces, necks, and breasts, were quite uncovered. The gardens and the baths of these Sultanas presented every degree of luxury and magnificence which Eastern taste has been able to invent.

Lady Montague had, perhaps, better opportunities of observing Turkish manners in private life, during her stay in that country, than any one who ever visited it. Her situation as the lady of our Ambassador, joined to her uncommon beauty and pleasing manners, made her company extremely acceptable to the Turkish ladies of the highest rank, and in one of her letters to her sister the Countess of Mar, she gives the following lively description of her reception at the palace of the fair Fatima, which is highly illustrative of Turkish customs.

"I was met at the door by two black eunuchs, who led me through a long gallery between two ranks of beautiful young girls, with their hair finely plaited, almost hanging to their feet, all dressed in fine white damasks, brocaded with silver. I was sorry that decency did not permit me to stop to consider them nearer. But that thought was lost upon my entrance into a large room, or rather pavilion, built round with gilded sashes, which were most of them thrown up, and the trees planted near them gave an agreeable shade, which hindered the sun from being troublesome. The jessamines and honeysuckles that twisted round their trunks gave a fine perfume, increased by a white marble fountain playing sweet water in the lower part of the room, which fell into three or four basins with a pleasing sonud. The roof was painted with all sorts of flowers, falling out of gilded baskets, that seemed tumbling down. On a sofa, raised three steps, and covered with fine Persian carpets, sat the *kiyaya's* (lieutenant-vizier) lady, leaning on cushions of white satin, embroidered; and at her feet sat two young girls about twelve years old, lovely as angels, dressed perfectly rich, and almost covered with jewels. But they were hardly seen near the fair *Fatima;* so much her beauty effaced every thing I have seen, nay, all that has been called lovely either in England or

Germany. I must own I never saw any thing so gloriously beautiful, nor can I recollect a face that would have been taken notice of near hers. She stood up to receive me, saluting me after their fashion, putting her hand to her heart with a sweetness full of majesty, that no court breeding could ever give. She ordered cushions to be given me, and took care to place me in the corner, which is the place of honour. I confess I was so struck with admiration, that I could not for some time speak to her, being wholly taken up in gazing. That surprising harmony of features! that charming result of the whole! that exact proportion of the body! that lovely bloom of complexion unsullied by art! the unutterable enchantment of her smile!—but her eyes!—large and black, with all the soft languishment of the blue! every turn of her face discovering some new grace.

"After my first surprise was over, I endeavoured, by nicely examining her face, to find out some imperfection, without any fruit of my search, but my being clearly convinced of the error of that vulgar notion, that a face exactly proportioned, and perfectly beautiful, would not be agreeable: nature having done for her with more success, what Apelles is said to have essayed by a collection of the most exact features, to form a perfect face. Add to all this a behaviour so full of grace and sweetness, such easy motions, with an air so majestic, yet free from stiffness or affectation, that I am persuaded, could she be suddenly transported upon the most polite throne of Europe, nobody would think her other than born and bred to be a queen, though educated in a country we call barbarous. To say all in word, our most celebrated English beauties would vanish near her.

"She was dressed in a *caftan* of gold brocade, flowered with silver, very well fitted to her shape, and showing to admiration the beauty of her bosom, only shaded by the thin gauze of her shift. Her drawers were pale pink, her waistcoat green and silver, her slippers white satin, finely embroidered; her lovely arms adorned with bracelets of diamonds, and her broad girdle set round with diamonds; upon her head a rich Turkish handkerchief of pink and silver, her own fine black hair hanging a great length in various tresses, and on one side of her head some bodkins. I am afraid you will accuse me of extravagance in this description. I think I have read somewhere that women always speak in rapture when they speak of beauty, and I cannot imagine why they should not be allowed to do so. For my part, I am not ashamed to own I took more pleasure in looking on the beauteous Fatima, than the finest piece of sculpture could have given me.

" She told me the two girls at her feet were her daughers, though she appeared too young to be their mother. Her fair maids were ranged below the sofa, to the number of twenty, and put me in mind of the ancient nymphs. I did not think all nature could have furnished such a scene of beauty. She made them a sign to play and dance. Four of them immediately began to play some soft airs on instruments between a lute and a guitar, which they accompanied with their voices, while the others danced by turns. This dance was very different from what I had seen before. Nothing could be more artful, or more proper, to raise *certain ideas.* The tunes so soft!—the motions so languishing!—accompanied with pauses and dying eyes! half falling back, and then recovering themselves in so artful a manner, that I am very positive the coldest and most rigid prude upon earth could not have looked upon them without thinking of *something not to be spoken of.* The music is extremely pathetic; 'tis true I am inclined to prefer the Italian, but perhaps I am partial. When the dance was over, four fair slaves came into the room with silver censers in their hands, and perfumed the air with amber, aloes-wood, and other scents. After this they served me coffee upon their knees in the finest china, with *soucoups* of silver, gilt. The lovely Fatima entertained me all this while in the most polite agreeable manner, calling me often *guzel sultanum*, or the beautiful sultana, and desiring my friendship with the best grace in the world, lamenting that she could not entertain me in my own language. When I took my leave, two maids brought in a fine silver basket of embroidered handkerchiefs; she begged I would wear the richest for her sake, and give the others to my women and interpretess. I retired through the same ceremonies as before, and could not help thinking I had been some time in Mahomet's Paradise, so much was I charmed with what I had seen."

This entertaining writer, in another letter to

her sister, gives the following interesting account of a bride's first visit to the bath.

" I was three days ago at one of the finest baths in the town, and had an opportunity of seeing a Turkish bride received there, and all the ceremony used upon such occasions, which made me recollect the epithalamium of Helen, by Theocritus; and it seems to me that the same customs have continued ever since. All the female friends and relations of the newly-allied families met at the bagnio, several others assembled out of curiosity; there were not less in the whole than two hundred. Those who were or had been married placed themselves round the rooms on marble sofas; but the virgins hastily undressed, having no other covering than their fine heads of hair; two of them met the bride at the door, to which she was conducted by her mother and another grave relation. She was a beautiful person about seventeen, very richly dressed, but soon reduced to a state of nature. Two others filled silver gilt pots with perfume, with which they scented the room. They then began the procession, following in pairs to the number of thirty, the leaders singing an epithalamium, answered in chorus by the others; the two last leading the bride, having her eyes fixed on the ground with a most charming air of modesty. In this order they walked round the three largest rooms in the bagnio. It is not easy to describe the beauty of this sight, most of them being well-proportioned, and finely skinned, which is improved by their frequent bathing. After having made the tour, they lead the bride to every one in the room, who compliments her either with a jewel or some other valuable present."

Lady Montague is of opinion, that the Turkish ladies enjoy more liberty than the European, for the following reasons. "No woman of what rank soever is ever permitted to go into the streets without being covered with two *mulins*, one that covers her face all but her eyes, the other that hides the whole dress of her head, and hangs half way down her back. Their shapes are also wholly concealed by an article of deep white they call a *ferigee*, which no woman of any sort appears without; this has straight sleeves that reach to the fingers' ends, and laps round them not unlike a riding-hood. You may guess then how effectual this disguises their persons, so that there is no distinguishing between the lady and her slave. It is impossible for the most jealous husband to know his wife when he meets her; and no man dare touch or follow a woman in the street. This perpetual masquerade gives them an entire liberty of following their inclinations without danger of discovery.

"The most usual method of intriguing is to send an appointment to the lover to meet the lady at a Jew's shop, which are as notoriously convenient as our Indian houses. The great ladies seldom let their gallants know who they are; and so difficult is it to find out, that they but very seldom can guess at her name, though they may have corresponded together for above half a year.

"You may easily imagine the number of faithful wives very small in a country where they have nothing to fear from a lover's indiscretion, since we see so many have the courage to expose themselves to that in this world, and all the threatened punishments in the next, which is never preached to the Turkish damsels. Neither have they much to apprehend from the anger of their husbands, those ladies that are rich having all their own money in their own hands. Upon the whole, I look upon the Turkish women as the only free people in the empire; the very divan pays respect to them; and the Grand Signior himself, when a pasha is executed, never violates the privileges of the harem, which remains unsearched and entire to the widow.

"They are queens of the slaves, whom the husband has not permission so much as to look upon, except it be an old woman or two whom the wife chooses. It is true their law permits them four wives, but there is no instance of a man of quality that makes use of this liberty, or of a woman of rank that would suffer it. When a husband happens to be inconstant, (which will sometimes happen,) he keeps his mistress in a house apart, and visits her as privately as possible, just as it is with you. Amongst all the great men here, I only know the *tefterdar*, (*i. e.* treasurer,) that keeps a number of she-slaves for his own use, that is to say on his own side of his house; for a slave, once given to serve a lady, is ever after at her disposal; and he is spoken of as a libertine, or what we should call a rake, if he were to interfere with them; and his wife won't see him, though she continues to live in his house."

As the Turks have it not in their power to leave their estates to any friend or even a distant relative, there is a custom very prevalent with them of adopting the child of some person, who from poverty or other cause are willing to part with them, and by this means they prevent their riches from falling into the treasury of the Grand Signior, who would otherwise claim them in default of issue by marriage. When they have adopted a child, they cite the parents before a magistrate, where they abjure all their future right or authority over the child, and the new parents charge themselves with the future care and education of it, adopting it as their own, and making it their lawful heir. A child thus adopted cannot be disinherited, yet there have been instances of common beggars who have refused to part with their children to the most opulent and powerful, so great is the instinctive affection natural to parents. The adopting parents are very tender to these *children of their souls*, as they call them.

Should a Christian be found intriguing with a

Turkish woman, he would be certainly put to death, even though the lady he was engaged with were not a married woman.

DALMATIA.—The Abbé Fortis, in his *Travels into Dalmatia*, gives us the following succinct account of the manners and marriage ceremony of the Morlacchi, and of some of the islands on the Coast of Dalmatia.

"The dress of the Morlack women is different in different parts of the country. That of the unmarried woman is the most complex and whimsical, in respect to the ornaments of the head; for when married they are not allowed to wear any thing else but a handkerchief, either white or coloured, tied about it. The girls use a scarlet cap, to which they commonly hang a veil falling down on the shoulder, as a mark of their virginity. The better sort adorn their caps with strings of silver coins, among which are very frequently seen very ancient and valuable ones; they have moreover earrings of very curious work, and small silver chains with the figures of half-moons fastened to the end of them. But the poor are forced to content themselves with plain caps, or, if they have any ornaments, they consist only of small exotic shells, round glass beads, or bits of tin. The principal merit of these caps, which constitute the good taste as well as vanity of the Morlock young ladies, is to attract and fix the eyes of all who are near them, by the multitude of ornaments, and the noise they make on the least motion of their heads. Hence half-moons of silver, or of tin, little chains and hearts, false stones and shells, together with all kinds of splendid trumpery, are readily admitted into their head-dress. In some districts they fix tufts of various coloured feathers, resembling two horns, on their caps; in others, artificial flowers, which they purchase in the sea-port towns; and it must be confessed, that, in the variety of those capricious and barbarious ornaments, sometimes a fancy not inelegant is displayed. Their holiday shifts are embroidered with silver and sometimes with gold, which they work themselves while they attend their flocks; and it is surprising to see how nicely this work is executed. Both old and young women wear about their necks large strings of round glass beads, of various size and colour; and many rings of brass, tin, or silver, on their fingers. Their bracelets are of leather, covered either with wrought tin or silver; and they embroider their stomachers, or adorn them with beads or shells. But the use of stays is unknown, nor do they put whalebone or iron in the stomacher. A broad woollen girdle surrounds their petticoat, which is commonly decked with shells and blue colour, and therefore called *modrina*. Their gown, as well as petticoat, is of a kind of serge, and both reach near to the ancle; the gown is bordered with scarlet, and called *sadak*. They use no *modrina* in summer, and only wear the *sadak* without sleeves over a linen petticoat or shift.—The girls always wear red stockings, and their shoes are like those of the men, called *opanke*. The sole is of undressed ox hide, and the upper part of the sheep's skin thongs knotted, which they call *apute* and these they fasten above the ancle, something like the ancient *coturnus*.

"The unmarried women, even of the richest families, are not permitted to wear any other sort of shoes; though after marriage they may, if they will, lay aside the *opanke*, and use Turkish slippers. The girls keep their hair tressed under their caps, but when married they let it fall dishevelled on their breast; sometimes they tie it under the chin; and always have medals, beads, or broad coins, in the Tartar or American mode, twisted amongst it. An unmarried woman, who falls under the imputation of want of chastity, runs the risk of having her red cap torn off her head publicly in church by the curate, and her hair cut by some relation, in token of infamy. Hence, if any of them happen to have fallen in an illicit amour, they commonly of their own accord lay aside the badge of virginity, and remove into another part of the country.

"Nothing is more common among the Morlacchi than marriages concluded between the old people of the respective families, especially when the parties live at a great distance, and neither see nor know each other; and the ordinary motive of these alliances is, the ambition of being related to a numerous and powerful family, famous for having produced valiant men. The father of the future bridegroom, or some other near relation of mature age, goes to ask the young woman, or rather the young woman of such a family, not having commonly any determinate choice. Upon this, all the girls of the house are shewn to him, and he chooses which pleases him best, though generally respecting the right of seniority. A denial in such cases is very rare, nor does the father of the maid enquire much into the circumstances of the family that asks her. Sometimes a daughter of the master is given in marriage to the servant, or tenant, as was usual in patriarchal terms; so little are the women regarded in this country. On these occasions, however, the Morlacchi girls enjoy a privilege which ours would also wish to have, as in justice they certainly ought. For he who acts by proxy, having obtained his suit, is obliged to go and bring the bridegroom; and if, on seeing each other, the young people are reciprocally content, the marriage is concluded, but not otherwise. In some parts, it is the custom for the bride to go to see the house and family of the proposed husband, before she gives a definitive answer; and, if the place or persons are disagreeable to her, she is at liberty to annul the contract. But, if she be contented, she returns to her father's house, escorted by the bridegroom and nearest relations. There the marriage day is appointed; on which the bridegroom comes to the bride's house, attended by all his friends of the greatest note, who, on the occasion, are called *Svati*, and are all armed, and on horseback, in their holiday clothes, with a peacock's feather in their cap, which is the distinctive ornament used by those who are invited to weddings. The company goes armed to repulse any attack, or ambush, that might be intended to disturb the feast. For, in old times, these encounters were not unfrequent, according to the records of many national heroic songs. In one of these is told the story of Janco Vojvod of Sebigne, who was contemporary with the famous George Castriotich, named Scanderbeg, and betrothed to Jagna of Temeswar, whose brothers, being not his friends, when he came to conclude the marriage, engaged him in the punctilio of performing certain feats, upon condition, that, if he succeeded, he was to have the bride, if not, he was to lose his life. These were, as the song relates, that he was to pierce an apple stuck on the point of a spear, with his dart, at a certain distance; then he was to spring over nine horses, placed one beside another, at one leap; and, lastly, to discover his future spouse among nine young women, all covered with veils. Janco, it seems, was a valiant soldier, but not expert in such trials of skill; however, his nephew undertook them in his place, and no objection was made. The expedient made use of by Zeculo, Janco's nephew, to know the bride among the other nine young women, was singular. He spread his mantle on the ground, threw a handful of gold rings on it, and then gallantly addressed the ladies as follows:—"Lovely maid, who art destined to be Janco's wife, do thou pick up these golden rings, and wear them; but if any other dares to touch one of them, I will cut off her arm at a blow." The nine young women were very naturally afraid of the danger, and did not choose to advance, so Janco's bride collected the rings, and thus the nuptial games were finished. When, upon trials of this nature, one of the parties found himself excluded, and another preferred, as he thought unjustly, he commonly had recourse to arms for redress, and much blood was often shed in those combats; and many tombs of the ancient Slavi are still to be seen in the woods and desert places of Morlacchia, whereon these feuds are engraved in coarse brass relief.

"The bride is conducted to a church, veiled and surrounded by the *Svati* on horseback, and the sacred ceremony is performed amidst the noise of muskets, pistols, barbaric shouts, and acclamations, which continue till she returns to her father's house, or to that of her husband, if not far off. Each of the *Svati* has his peculiar inspection, as well during the cavalcade, as at the marriage feast, which begins immediately on their return from church. The *Parvinax* precedes all the rest, singing such songs as he thinks most suitable to the occasion. The *Bariactar* brandishes a lance with a silken banner fastened to it, and an apple stuck on the point: there are two *Bariactars*, and sometimes four, at the more noble marriages. The *Stari-svat* is the principal personage of the brigade, and the most respectable relation is commonly invested with this dignity. The *Stacheo's* duty is to receive and obey the orders of the *Stari-svat*. The two *Diveri*, who ought to be the bridegroom's brothers, when he has any, are appointed to serve the bride. The *Knum* corresponds to our sponsors; and the *Komorgia*, or *Seksaña*, is deputed to receive and guard the dowry. A *Ciaous* carries the mace, and attends to the order of the march, as master of the ceremonies; he goes singing aloud, *Breberi*, *Davori*, *Dobrastichia*, *Jura*, *Pico*, names of ancient propitious deities. *Buklia* is the cupbearer of the company, as well on the march as at table; and all these officers are doubled, and sometimes tripled, in proportion to the number of the company.

"The first day's entertainment is sometimes made at the bride's house, but generally at the bridegroom's, whither the *Svati* hasten immediately after the nuptial benediction; and, at the same time, three or four men run on foot to tell the good news; the first who gets to the house has a kind of towel, embroidered at the ends, as a premium. The *Domachin*, or head of the house, comes out to meet his daughter-in-law, and a child is handed to her before she alights, to caress it; and, if there happen to be none in the house, the child is borrowed from one of the neighbours. When she alights, she kneels down and kisses the threshold. Then the mother-in-law, or in her place some other female relation, presents a corn-sieve full of different kinds of grain, nuts, almonds, and other small fruit, which the bride scatters upon the *Svati* by handfuls behind her back. The bride does not sit at the table the first day, but has one apart for herself, the two *Diveri*, and the *Stacheo*. The bridegroom sits at table with the *Svati*, but in all that day, consecrated to the matrimonial union, he must neither unloose nor cut any thing whatever. The *Knum* carves his meat, and cuts his bread. It is the *Domachin's* business to give the toasts; and the *Stari-svat* is the first who pledges him. Generally the *Bukkara*, a very large wooden cup, goes round, first to the Saint Protector of the family; next to the prosperity of the holy faith; and sometimes to a name the most sublime and venerable. The most extravagant abundance reigns at the feasts, and each of the *Svati* contributes by sending a share of provisions.—The dinner begins with fruit and cheese, and the soup comes last, just contrary to our custom. All sorts of domestic fowls, kid, lamb, and sometimes venison, are heaped in prodigal quantities upon their tables. The women relations, if they be invited, never dine at table with the men, it being an established custom for them to dine by themselves. After dinner, they pass the rest of the day in dancing, singing ancient songs, and in games of dexterity, or of wit and fancy; and in the evening, at a convenient hour after supper, the three ritual healths having first gone round, the *Knum* accompanies the bridegroom to the matrimonial apartment, which commonly is the cellar or the stable, whither the bride is also conducted by the *Diveri*, and the *Stacheo;* but the three last are obliged to retire, and the *Knum* remains alone with the new-married couple. If there happen to be any bed prepared better than straw, he leads them to it, and, having untied the bride's girdle, he causes them both to undress each other reciprocally. It is not long since the *Knum* was obliged to undress the bride entirely, but that custom is now out of use; and, instead of it, he has the privilege of kissing her, as often as he pleases, wherever he meets her; which privilege may possibly be agreeable for the first months, but must soon become very disgusting. When they are both undressed, the *Knum* retires, and stands listening at the door, if there be a door. It is his business to announce the consummation of the marriage, which he does by discharging a pistol, and is answered by many of the company. The next day the bride, without her veil and virginal cap, dines at table with the *Svati*, and is forced to hear the coarse equivocal jests of her indelicate and sometimes intoxicated company.

"The nuptial feasts, called *Sdrave* by the ancient Huns, are by our Morlacchi called the *Sdravize*, from whence the Italian word *Stravizzo* is undoubtedly derived. They continue three, six, eight, or more days, according to the ability or prodigal disposition of the family where they are held. The new married wife gets no inconsiderable profit in these days of joy, and it usually amounts to much more than all the portion which she brings with her, which often consists of nothing but her own clothes, and perhaps a cow; nay, it happens sometimes that the parents, instead of giving money with their daughter, get something from the bridegroom by way of price. The bride carries water every morning to wash the hands of her guests as long as the feasting lasts, and each of them throws a small piece of money into the bason after performing that function, which is indeed a very rare one among them, excepting on such occasions. The bride is also permitted to raise other little contributions among the

Svati, by hiding their shoes, caps, knives, or some other necessary part of their equipage, which they are obliged to ransom by a piece of money, according as the company rates it. And, besides all these voluntary or extorted contributions already mentioned, each guest must give some present to the new-married wife at taking leave the last day of the *Sdravize*, and then she also distributes some trifles in return, which commonly consists in shirts, caps, handkerchiefs, and such like.

"The nuptial rites are almost precisely the same through all the vast country inhabited by the Morlacchi, and those in use among the peasantry and common people of the sea-coast of Dalmatia, Istria, and the islands, differ but little from them. Yet, among these particular varieties, there is one of the island Zlarine, near Sebenico, remarkable enough; for there the *Stari-svat* (who may naturally be supposed to be drunk at that hour) must, at one blow with his naked broad sword, strike the bride's crown of flowers off her head, when she is ready to go to bed. And in the island of Pago, in the village of Novoglia, there is a custom more comical and less dangerous, but equally savage and brutal. After the marriage contract is settled, and the bridegroom comes to conduct his bride to church, her father or mother, in delivering her over to him, makes an exaggerated enumeration of her ill qualities: 'Know, since thou wilt have her, that she is good for nothing, ill-natured, obstinate, &c.' On which the bridegroom, affecting an angry look, turns to the young woman, with an 'Ah! since it is so, I will teach you to behave better;' and at the same time regales her with a blow or a kick, or some piece of similar gallantry, which is by no means figurative. And it seems in general that the Morlack women, and perhaps the greatest part of the Dalmatians, the inhabitants of the cities excepted, do not dislike a beating either from their husbands or lovers.

"In the neighbourhood of Dernish the women are obliged, during the first year after marriage, to kiss all their relational acquaintances who come to the house; but, after the first year, they are dispensed from that compliment; and, indeed, they become so intolerably nasty, that they are no longer fit to practise it. Perhaps the mortifying manner in which they are treated by their husbands and relations is at the same time both the cause and effect of this shameful neglect of their persons. When a Morlack husband mentions his wife, he always premises, by your leave, or begging your pardon. And when the husband has a bedstead, the wife must sleep on the floor near it. I have often lodged in Morlack houses, and observed that the female sex is universally treated with contempt; it is true that the women are by no means amiable in that country; they even deform and spoil the gifts nature.

"The pregnancy and births of these women would be thought very extraordinary among us, where the ladies suffer so much, notwithstanding all the care and circumspection used before and after labour. On the contrary, a Morlack woman neither changes her food nor interrupts her daily fatigue on account of her pregnancy, and is frequently delivered in the fields, or in the road by herself, and takes the infant, washes it in the first water she finds, carries it home, and returns the day after to her usual labour, or to feed her flock. The custom of the nation is invariable in washing the new-born infants in cold water.

Among the Morlacchi also a kind of Platotonic union sometimes takes place, which is similar to what we term sworn brothers or sisters. These engagements are entered into before the altar, between men and men, and women and women. They promise to assist each other in their mutual necessities, their jealousies, and wrongs; and, indeed, they seldom violate those friendly contracts, which they hold so sacred, that the breach of them by any one is talked of with detestation and horror over the whole country.

ASIA.

PERSIA, ARMENIA, & SIAM.

THE Persians, says Chardin, regard it as a tenet of their religion that a man ought to guard both his faith and his wives with equal vigilance, and that it is criminal in him merely to look at the *habitations* of his neighbours' wives. Their jealousy is carried to such a pitch, that, when they inter their women, they erect a hut over the grave, that no man may see even the lifeless remains. They instil into the minds of females, from their earliest infancy, that the greatest virtue and honour consist, not only in avoiding the society of the other sex, but also in equally avoiding the sight of them. They believe that the faithful in Paradise will have eyes in the crown of their head, that they may not see the *houris* or celestial women who belong to others. A married woman, who is not of the lowest class, is not permitted to see her nephews, or her husband's brothers, any more than strangers; her acquaintance with the other sex being confined to her husband and her own sons; brothers are invariably denied access to their sisters. When the women pay visits, a number of horsemen ride before and behind, crying *Kuruck! Kuruck!* which is equivalent to ordering all males within hearing to avoid coming in the way; for, should a man by any inadvertence be found near, the eunuchs who guard the procession would immediately chastise him with their staves, without his being able to obtain any remedy. But nothing excites greater terror in Persia than this alarming exclamation before the women of the king, every unfortunate who is found being put to death.— This circuit extends as far as the camels can be discerned that are employed in drawing or carrying the equipage. When the route of the royal harem is known, all the male inhabitants near where it is to pass must quit their houses. When Chardin was in Persia, the harem of the young monarch paid frequent visits to the country during the first two years of his reign, and the train invariably traversed the suburbs of Ispahan, to clear the intended road of men. The king's concubines sometimes left the seraglio at night, when all males in the route were obliged to leave their beds and get out of the way, whether sick or well, old or young, let the weather or roads be ever so bad. When the harem travels in the country, the attendants are employed for half a day at least before they set out in clearing the roads they are to pass; a whole regiment of cavalry is employed to perform this duty. The first notice is not considered as sufficient; for, two hours before they set off, the guards again scour the roads, and by incessant discharges of musquetry announce the expected arrival of the cavalcade. Not content with these precautions, the white eunuchs, one hour before their departure, sally forth to see that the road is clear and safe, for, should they meet with a man, he would be immediately dispatched, let him be ever so old, imbecile, or infirm, in body or mind. Chardin records several examples of men losing their lives, who, on account of their great age, conceived themselves entitled to the rights of eunuchs, and approached the person of the monarch to deliver petitions of travellers who were ignorant of the passing of the harem and of the servants of the king, who had fallen asleep through fatigue, who suffered either by the hand of the despot himself, or by his executioners. In the same writer's time, women were forbidden to appear in the way of the king, because Abbas II. had taken a beautiful Armenian from her husband, which would not have taken place but for her being seen by the king. At that time this was the only instance that could be recollected of the king taking away the wife of another, in violation of the most sacred laws of Mahomet. It is true the Persian laws allow that whatever is touched by the king still remains immaculate, and that he may go into the harem of any of his subjects; but the captain of the guard to the harem of the commander-in-chief of the armies of Abbas the Great once had the courage to tell the king, one day after dinner, when he signified his intention of going to repose in his general's harem, that he would not admit any beard but his master's into the seraglio he had the charge of. The king asked him if he knew to whom he was speaking; the undaunted warrior replied, "To the king of men, but not to the king of women;" which reply, instead of exciting the king's displeasure, procured the captain a handsome reward for his courage.

In Persia, when the parents of a young man have determined upon marrying him, *they* look out among their kindred and acquaintance for a proper match; they then go to the house where the female lives; if her father approves, he orders sweetmeats to be brought, which is a direct sign of compliance. After this, the usual presents on the part of the bridegroom are made, which, if the person be in middling circumstances, generally consists of two complete suits of apparel of the best sort, a ring, a looking-glass, and a small sum of money, which is to provide for her in case of a divorce. The contract is witnessed by the cadi, or magistrate. On the wedding-night the bride is brought forth, covered from head to foot in a veil of red silk or painted muslin; a horse is then sent by the bridegroom for her to mount; a looking-glass is held before her (all the way to the bridegroom's house) by one of the bridesmaids, as an admonition to her that it is the last time she will look therein a virgin. A numerous procession follows, and the rejoicings generally last for eight or ten days. Men marry either for life or a determined time. Travellers or merchants who intend staying any time generally apply to the magistrate for a wife during their residence, when the cadi, for a stated gratuity, produces a number of girls, whom he declares to be honest and healthy, and he becomes surety for them. It is said that, among thousands, there is not one instance of dishonesty during the time agreed upon.

The Persians may marry four wives, and keep as many concubines as they please. The women, indeed, are generally treated and considered as little better than slaves, being absolutely prisoners; and, among the lower order, they till the land, plant rice, and do every kind of field as well as domestic work, while their husbands go to market, smoke their pipes, or saunter about.

The ancient Persians entertained an opinion that those who were or had been married enjoyed a superior state of felicity hereafter, and therefore frequently hired persons to be espoused to such of their relations as died in a state of celibacy.

There is no such thing as bastardy in Persia, the children of slaves and concubines inheriting equally with those born in wedlock.

The *Gaurs*, a religious sect of Persia, never

intermarry with any other sect. They only allow of one wife, prohibiting concubines and divorces, unless a wife continue barren for nine years, when they are permitted to take another.

ARMENIA.—Pouqueville gives the following ludicrous description of an Armenian and a Turkish marriage which took place at Pera while he resided there, at which he was present. —"I once saw a strange procession pass by, which they informed me was an Armenian wedding, and I took care to have the characters explained to me as they passed by, so sorrowful and grave did they appear. The march commenced by fiddlers and flute-players, (who made a most dreadful and unharmonious squeaking,) with dancers, who sang and tripped it at the same time; they were followed by a groupe of relations; next to them a body of men with torches of yellow wax, who seemed as if escorting a funeral; immediately afterwards the bride was seen, supported by two of her nearest relations; a sack was drawn over her head down to her feet; but, in order that her respiration should not be checked, they put a wooden platter or tea-board upon her head, by which the sack was kept from her mouth and nostrils. She was separated from the bridegroom by a party of guests. He then came alone, enveloped in napkins, with his arms crossed and placed on his breast; his head was covered with a silk shawl, and inclined on the left shoulder, while his long whiskers and remarkable appearance gave rather the idea of a criminal about to receive punishment than a bridegroom about to receive the hymeneal crown. Behind him, I know not for what reason, came two Armenians, holding in their hands two rusty sabres, of which they appeared to be in dread, and raising them from time to time in a menacing attitude towards heaven; the rest of the relations followed at a melancholy and slow pace. As the ceremony took place in my neighbourhood, I had an opportunity of observing that the good Armenians did not lose their time in vague ceremonies, for the banquet degenerated into a most scandalous orgie, which lasted without interruption for three days and three nights.

"The form of a Turkish wedding, which I witnessed some time afterwards, afforded me more entertainment by its variety and the events with which it was attended. The procession passed through Asia into Europe in the elegant casques, or barges, of Constantinople, which scarcely seem to touch the waves. The young bride, covered with a veil, and surrounded by women, occupied a boat with four oars; several others were filled with instrumental performers, and in those which led the van were two buffoons, who were seated on the poop; they blew a kind of horn, and frisked about, and often made a high jump, which occasioned the boat to heel in such a manner as at length to upset, when the mimics and their company were in an instant ten feet under water, which did not seem to give any concern to those about them. They however soon re-appeared on the surface, and, in the most ludicrous manner imaginable, vomited up the water they had swallowed; they then clung to the boat till it came to the shore, where they arrived with downcast looks. As to the watermen, having righted their boat, they cursed the buffoons and the wedding, following the procession in order to get paid for their trouble."

The Armenian clergy are allowed to marry, but they are not allowed to say mass for the space of seven days after their nuptials, and when they are allowed they must be shut up in the church five days previous, and five days subsequent thereto, during which time they must have nothing to live upon but vegetables and water. A second marriage totally incapacitates them from officiating ever after. A father is prohibited marrying with a god-child; nor can ever those marry who are of different families, if they happen to have the same godfather. The Armenian's children are all married during their infancy, which is a political precaution to preserve them from being sent to the emperor's seraglio, or harems of the grandees; the Persians being particular in avoiding adultery, or depriving a man of his wife. Though the contract is thus made in infancy, the cohabitation is not allowed until a suitable age. —The bridegroom annually makes the bride a present at Easter, consisting of a fine silk garment, &c. prior to the celebration of the nuptials.

Among the Georgians some follow the Armenian custom of marrying their children while infants, that their lords or governors may not take the girls for concubines; but this is only to be understood of those who have a larger share of decency than the generality of them.

Siam.——Among the Siamese and many other nations of Asia, the legitimate wife is considered and treated as the mother of all the children of her husband's other wives or concubines, and as such receives their duty and respects; the children being taught so from their infancy, they show no regret at the loss of their natural mother, nor for the sufferings she may endure, but receive her attendance as that of a servant. The legitimate wife and her children frequently, at the death of the husband, drive away and dispossess the concubines, or more properly the other wives, the only distinction being either priority of bearing a son or in marriage. Sometimes the wife, if she choose, will take all the children, and drive away their mothers, in which the children always coincide; at other times she will only retain some of them, turning out the rest with their unhappy mothers, destitute and friendless upon the world.—Such are the barbarous customs of many Asiatics, that the children feel no reluctance at seeing their parents sold for slaves, as they frequently are in Siam. When husband and wife are divorced, they divide the children in such a manner, that the first, third, fifth, and so on, go to the wife, the husband taking the second, fourth, sixth, and so on. If there be only one, the wife has a right thereto.

The Siamese women are under few restraints; they marry early, being past parturition at forty. The espousals are concluded by female mediators; and, as wealth is carefully concealed, from dread of extortion by the prince or magistrate, a magician is consulted concerning the propriety of the alliance. On the third visit, after the exchange of a few presents, the parties are considered as united. Polygamy is allowed, but rather practised from ostentation, and one wife is always acknowledged as supreme. From pride, the royal marriages are sometimes incestuous, the king not hesitating to marry his own sister. Divorce is tolerated on condition that the husband return the portion that his wife brought him, but is seldom practised, as mutual necessities and habits perpetuate the union of the poor; the rich can choose a more complaisant mistress without dismissiug the former. Temporary intercourse is rather forbidden by the pride of the sex than by any legal or moral obligation, it being regarded as a brief marriage, and inconstancy as a divorce.

HINDOSTAN, CHINA, & TARTARY.

The Hindoos regard it as an irrefragable principle, that women were created for no other purpose than the gratification of man and producing children. Not only do the Orientals neither expect nor reverence any virtue in woman, but they ascribe to them, without exception, every vice of which the sex is capable, and by which it is most debased. The appetite of a woman, say the laws of the Hindoos, can no more be satiated than a devouring fire by the combustibles that are thrown into it; or the ocean by the rivers which discharge themselves into its bosom; or the empire of death by the men and animals that it swallows up. Woman, continues the genius of Hindostanic legislation, has six inherent failings; in the first place, an inordinate love of dress, finery, and delicacies; in the second, an immoderate love of sensual pleasures; thirdly, a violent irascibility; fourthly, a profound and dissembled malice; fifthly, an innate jealousy, which converts the good qualities of others into bad; sixthly, a natural inclination to evil—a sentiment that conveys more than the other five.

Some of the *Nairs*, or nobles of Hindostan, have the strange custom of one wife being in common with about half a dozen of them; the number is not limited by any law, but by a sort of tacit consent. They cohabit in turn, according to priority of marriage; and when one is with the wife, he leaves his arms at the door, as a signal for no one to enter. They marry in their childhood, and some of the higher ranks of Gentoos take several wives. The little bride and bridegroom are carried through the streets for several successive nights, dressed in the most elegant stile, the houses being at the same time illuminated, and preceded by their relatives and friends, with music playing and streamers flying. They all proceed to the house of the bride's father, and the little couple being seated opposite to each other, separated by a table, across which they join their hands, the priest puts a kind of hood upon the head of each, and, supplicating heaven to prosper them, they receive the nuptial benediction, and this concludes the ceremony.

The women begin to bear children at about

the age of twelve, and treat their husbands with the most profound respect, affection, and tenderness, being entirely in their power. They bring no other portion than their clothes, or a few female slaves; yet they enjoy more freedom than the wives of the Mahometans. The distinguishing characteristic of a Gentoo married lady is fidelity to her husband.

The reason assigned by the Gentoos for women burning themselves on the funeral pile of their husband is, that formerly the women freed themselves from an unpleasant partner by poison, which induced the legislature to provide for the safety of husbands, by a remedy as odious as the evil, by forcing the women to burn themselves on his funeral pile.

The Hindoo laws declare it to be adultery, though of a less criminal nature, if a man look at, nod to, or smile, at a married woman; or if he enter into conversation, either in the morning or evening; or remain in a garden, or other retired place. A second and more criminal species of adultery with them is a man sending presents of any description to a married woman. But, upon the whole, they punish adultery with less severity than is exercised upon females of a superior cast having illicit connection with a man of inferior cast; but a man of superior cast may, with impunity, attach himself to a female of inferior cast.

The Druses are so excessively jealous, that, if a man were to inform his friend of the health of the female branches of his own family, and to inquire after the other's wife or daughter, the inquiry or intelligence would irritate a Druse to that degree, that he would go home and put his wife and daughter to death, as persons who were a disgrace to him, and seize the first opportunity of dispatching his inquisitive or officious acquaintance. Enquiries and accounts, which in Europe pass for nothing, or at most bespeak attention and respect, are certainly fraught with much more meaning in Asia than in our quarter of the globe.

When a Bramin hears of the promiscuous conversation between the sexes in Europe, he generally replies with the following proverb: "If you set butter in the sun, you must expect it to melt," which, in Asia, may perhaps be verified.

The Bramins marry their children very young, especially the richer persons; many about their eighth year, and some in their fifth. A Bramin takes especial notice of all things that he meets with in the way, when he is going to choose a wife for his son, and, as often as he meets with any thing that is ominous or unfortunate, so often he returns and defers his intent. After the consent of both parties is obtained, a day is appointed for the celebration of the marriage; and they are very particular in choosing what they esteem a lucky day. When the day is come, they kindle the fire *homam*, which is made with the wood of a consecrated tree, called *rawasittow*, and a priest repeats several prayers. After this, the bridegroom takes three handfuls of rice, which he throws on the bride's head, who does the same to him; which done, the bride's father, according to his circumstances, adorns the bride, and also washes the feet of the bridegroom, and puts ornaments upon him. Then the father, taking his daughter by the hand, puts it into the water with which he washed the bridegroom's feet, and, in the name of God, gives him the money, at the same time saying, "*I have nothing more to do with you; I hereby give her to you.*" When the father gives his daughter's hand to the bridegroom, he also gives a jewel, called *sali*, which has a golden head of an idol fixed to it, and, being suspended by a string, is shown to all present, and after some prayers and good wishes is tied round the bride's neck by the hands of the bridegroom, by which the marriage is confirmed.

CHINA.——Courtship and marriage, among the opulent classes in China, is conducted in the following summary manner. The young people are not suffered to see each other, or treat upon the subject of their nuptials; the parents settle every thing themselves, and, though in other countries it is the custom for women to bring portions to their husbands, here the husband pays a sum of money to the bride, which is generally laid out in clothes, &c. for her. Then follow certain ceremonies, the chief of which consist in the relations on both sides sending to demand the name of the intended bride and bridegroom, and making them presents. The parents of the bride, who fix the period of the nuptials, frequently consult the calendar for a propitious day; and in the mean time the man sends his bride some jewels or trinkets, or what he can afford.

On the day appointed for the celebration of

the nuptials, the bride is put into a sedan, which is magnificently adorned with festoons of artificial flowers, and her baggage of clothes, ornaments, and trinkets, are carried after her in chests by her servants, or other persons hired for the purpose, with lighted flambeaux, though it be noon day; the sedan is preceded by music, and followed by the relations and friends of the bride. The nearest relation carries in his hand the key of the sedan, (for the windows of it are grated up and locked,) and gives it to the bridegroom as soon as the procession reaches his house, who waits at his door in order to receive her. As this is the first interview between the bride and bridegroom, it is easy to conceive with what eager curiosity he opens the door of the sedan. It sometimes happens that he is dissatisfied with his lot; when he immediately shuts the door again, and sends her back to her friends, choosing rather to lose his money than be united to a person he does not like; this, however, is seldom the case.

As soon as the bride steps out of her chair, the bridegroom presents her his hand, and leads her into a hall, where a table is set for them in particular; the rest of the company sit at other tables, the men in one apartment of the hall, the women in another; but, before the bride and bridegroom sit down, they make four reverences to *Tien*, a spirit which they suppose resides in heaven. When seated at table, they pour wine on the ground before they begin to eat, and set apart some of the provisions for their idols. The moment each of them tastes the viands on the table, the bridegroom rises up and invites his lady to drink, upon which she rises also and returns the compliment. After this two cups of wine are brought, of which they drink part, and pour the residue into another cup, of which they drink alternately; this latter part of the ceremony ratifies the nuptials. The bride then goes among the ladies, and spends the remainder of the day with them: the bridegroom treats his friends in a separate apartment. In China, it would be as preposterous to appear in white at a wedding, as it would in Europe to be in black. No Chinese, except the emperor, can have more than one wife, but he may have as many concubines as he pleases; but they must be obedient to the wife, and treat her as mistress. The emperor has three wives, and the number of concubines are estimated at three hundred. If a wife elope from her husband she is sentenced to be whipped, and he may dispose of her as a slave; should she marry another whilst her first husband is living, he is at liberty to have her strangled. If a man quit his wife and family, the wife, after three years, may apply to the mandarin, and, upon stating her situation, he can authorise her to take another husband; she, however, would be severely punished were she to marry without this permission. In certain cases a man may turn off his wife; as for instance, if she be barren, for a bad temper, theft, or any contagious disorder. Divorces are very rare among the rich, and the poor practice it but seldom, though there are some instances of it among both.

At Tonquin, where fruitfulness is honoured, the pain imposed on barren wives is to search for agreeable girls and bring them to their husbands. In consequence of this political institution, the Tonquinese think the Europeans ridiculous in having only one wife; and cannot conceive why, among us, rational beings can think of honouring God by a vow of chastity. They maintain, that, when there is an opportunity, it is as criminal not to give life to what has it not, as to take it from those who already have it.

The Chinese have the power of selling their daughters to wife to whom they please, and if the father of the girl gives a dowry with her, she is looked upon as the superior female in her husband's house. Some fathers will (like the Calmacs, their progenitors) sell their children, upon condition of its being a female, while the mother is yet pregnant.

Among the Chinese, a son dare not refuse the wife his father has chosen for him, any more than the daughter can refuse the husband her father has chosen for her, even though they never saw or heard of each other before.

TARTARY.—Among the *Thibetians* in Chinese Tartary, polygamy, according to our conception of the word, is not practised here; but it exists in a manner still more repugnant to European ideas. A plurality of husbands is highly respected. It is usual in Thibet for the brothers of a family to have a wife in common, and they generally live in harmony and comfort with her, though sometimes dissentions will arise; an instance of which Mr. Bogle mentions in the case of a modest and virtuous lady, the wife of half a dozen of the Tayshoo-Lama's nephews, who complained to the uncle that the two youngest of her husbands did not pay her that attention which duty and religion required of them. Sometimes a man confines himself to one wife, and a woman to one husband.

The marriage ceremonies are neither tedious nor intricate in Thibet. Their courtships are carried on with little art, and quickly brought to a conclusion. The man makes a proposal to the parents of a damsel, who, if they approve of the match, repair to his house, where the male and female friends of both parties meet and carouse for three days, having music, dancing, &c. at the expiration of which time the marriage is complete. The priests of Thibet have no part in the contract, as they studiously shun the company of women. Mutual consent is their only bond of union; but the husband or wife cannot separate themselves, unless, indeed, the same sentiment which joined them induce a separation; but, in those cases, they are not at liberty to form a new alliance. Incontinency is punished by corporeal punishment in the woman; the man expiates his transgression by a pecuniary fine.

The ceremony of marriage among the *Calmucs* is performed on horseback. The girl is first mounted, who rides off at full speed; her lover pursues, and, if he overtake her, she becomes his wife, and the marriage is consummated on the spot. They then return to his tent. It sometimes happens that the woman does not wish to be married to the man who pursues her, in which case she will not suffer him to overtake her: and we are assured that no instance occurs of a Calmuc girl being overtaken, unless she has a partiality to her pursuer.

It is a frequent practice with this tribe to betroth their children while the mother is yet pregnant, on condition of its being a girl, the father having the absolute power of disposing of his daughters in marriage; but they generally give for their dowry as much as they received for their price. They have several women; but the first, or she only who brings a dowry, is considered as the wife, being sanctioned by the priest, the other being obliged to pay obeisance to her.

The wife of a Calmuc, while remaining at home, is a sort of inviolable character, no one daring to attack her; nay, she may even throw dirt, stones, &c. or abuse passers-by, without their daring to molest or prevent her so doing, provided she continues in her husband's house, otherwise she would most assuredly meet with very severe retaliation.

The Calmuc Priests are not suffered to have wives; but they may pass a night with any man's wife, which is esteemed a favour by the husband.

When a *Mingrelian* wishes to take a wife, he must purchase her. A tolerable good price is given for a virgin, and considerable less for a woman who has been divorced. When the contract is made, the couple are immediately at liberty to cohabit together previous to payment of the money. They can divorce their wives either for barrenness or ill-nature.

The ancient *Thracians* entertained very different notions with respect to chastity before marriage; but conjugal infidelity they considered as an unpardonable offence.

The politic Gengiz-Khan, in order to reconcile those deadly feuds so prevalent among different tribes of the Tartars, instituted the ceremony of marriage between a young man and a young woman (who had been some time deceased) of two hostile tribes; and those tribes, by this imaginary union, were very frequently reconciled and brought into habits of intercourse and friendship, when every other method had been tried in vain.—This ideal contract was regarded with the most superstitious veneration, and any breach of it, whenever it had taken place, was considered as a most alarming omen.

ASIATIC ISLANDS.

In Ceylon the marriage ceremonies of the Chingulays are somewhat similar to those of many of the Tartar tribes. The man first sends to her whom he wishes to become his wife, to purchase her clothes, which she freely sells for a stipulated sum. In the evening he carries them to her, sleeps with her all night, and in the morning they appoint the day of marriage, on which he provides two courses, one for the friends of each party. The feast is held at the bride's dwelling, where the couple eat out of the same dish, their thumbs are tied together, and they sleep together that night, and on the following morning go to the bridegroom's house, which concludes the ceremony. Afterwards the husband eats alone, the wife all the time waiting upon him; and when he is done, then she is allowed to sit down, and her children with her, to partake of what is left.

The reason of their purchasing the bride's clothes is that she and her relations may be satisfied with respect to the man's circumstances, as she always asks as much as she thinks requisite for them to begin the world with.

They are permitted to part from each other whenever they please, and so frequently do they avail themselves of this privilege, that they often change a dozen times before their inclination is entirely suited. If a woman is heard to mention the name of the King, her tongue is immediately cut out. The manner in which the female salutes is by clapping her hands together, and bringing them so closed to her head.

In the Island of JAVA, when a couple is married, the friends of each party borrow as many ornaments as they can to adorn the bride and bridegroom. The festivity continues sometimes a fortnight, or longer, during which time the bridegroom is not even permitted to see the bride.

Being descendants of the Chinese, all their ceremonies are nearly similar.

When a Javanese lady marries, she throws all her dolls, childish trinkets, &c. into the fire, to evince her determination to become a woman. The company then congratulate her on her marriage, and make her several valuable presents, to recompense her for those she has destroyed.

The Javanese are so very jealous of their wives, that they will not permit their grown up sons to see their own mothers.

When any of the Emperor's women are convicted of infidelity, they are executed in the following manner:—The writer of this account says, that at the time he resided at Java, there were thirteen of the Emperor's wives to suffer death for this crime. "It was in the forenoon, about eleven of the clock, when the fair criminals were led into an open space within the palace; the judge passed sentence upon them, by which they were to be poisoned with a lance, dipped in *upas*. An Alcoran was then presented to them, and they were forced to confess, according to the Mahometan laws, that the sentence passed upon them was just and equitable. This they did by laying their right hand upon the Alcoran, their left upon their breast, and having their eyes lifted towards heaven; the judge then held the Alcoran to their lips, and they kissed it. These ceremonies over, the executioner proceeded on his business in the following manner:—Thirteen posts, each about five feet high, had been previously erected; to these the delinquents were fastened, and their bosom bared. They continued a short time in prayer, attended by several priests, until the signal was made by the judge to the executioner, when the latter produced an instrument much like the spring lances used by farriers to bleed horses. With this instrument, which was poisoned with the gum of the *upas*, the unhappy creatures were pierced in the middle of the breast; and the operation was performed on all of them in less than two minutes.

"My astonishment was raised to the highest degree on perceiving the sudden effects of the poison; for, in less than five minutes, they were all seized with a violent tremor, attended with a *subsultus tendinum;* after which they died in the greatest agonies, calling upon God and Mahomet to have mercy upon them: and in sixteen minutes they had all expired. Upon examining the bodies some time after, they were full of livid spots, like those of the *petechiæ*, their faces much swoln, their colour changed to a kind of a blue, and their eyes yellow."

In the LADRONES, the men were formerly governed by their wives, the women assuming those prerogatives which in most other countries are invested in the other sex, and were regarded as though they were queens or sacred priestesses of the great national deity. We are informed by Gobien, that the wife is absolute mistress in her house, the husband not daring to dispose of any thing without her consent. If she disapprove of his conduct in general or his treatment of her in particular, she wreaks her vengeance upon him, or abandons him entirely. On a separation of this kind, the wife takes all the property and children with her, they being taught to consider the new husband which she may choose as their father.

If the wife were guilty of adultery, the husband might revenge himself how he pleased on the adulterer; but on no account was he allowed to molest his wife. If the wife had reason to suspect the fidelity of her husband, she might amply revenge herself, either by summoning all the women of the village, or appealing to her own relations. In the last case, the females, with their husbands' hats on, and spears in their hands, proceed to the habitation of the guilty or suspected husband; they commence their operations by ravaging his land and destroying the produce thereof; they then attack and destroy his house, and, if they find him, they treat him in the most barbarous manner. The relations, if she appeal to them, pursue a similar line of conduct. The dread of such usage frequently deterred many young men from entering into the married state, and induced them to club together and purchase a woman or women of some other country, toward the support of which they each contributed; and hence arose the custom among them of a community of wives. Whence the women derived their authority is hard to guess, the men there being as robust as any of the natives of the East India or South Sea Islands.

In the Island of MACASSAR, as soon as the priest has performed the marriage ceremony, the bridegroom and bride are locked up in an apartment together for three successive days, having a person to bring what necessaries they may have occasion for; the friends and relations during the above time being feasted and entertained at the house of the bride's father. At the expiration of the three days they are liberated; and receive the congratulations of their friends. The bridegroom then conducts the bride to his home, and they pursue their ordinary avocations, she to the duty of housewifery, he to his customary profession.

The law permits them to marry at the age of fifteen, but they seldom marry until thoroughly trained to the use of arms, of which a respectable author gives this narration :—"During the time of the war between the inhabitants of Dungally and Parlow, a piratical prow arrived at Dungally from Magindano, or Mindaneo; she was owned by a Rajah, named Tomba, who was an elderly man, and was on board with his son, who was about twenty years of age. The son of Rajah Tomba saw the daughter of Tooa, late Rajah of Dungally, but who had resigned his government in favour of his son Arvo. The young man fell in love with the Rajah's daughter, and applied to Taun Hadjee for his assistance. The priest was employed in the negociation for several days, when it was agreed that the young man, or his father, should give three brass swivel guns, and twenty pieces of white cloth, which was reckoned a great dowry. The parties were all taken to the *longar*, or court-house, and examined, before the marriage could be celebrated. On the day appointed for the marriage, all the warriors of the place were armed; and about one in the afternoon the young man, with his father, and all the men belonging to the prow, armed as if for an engagement, came on shore. Tuan Hadjee and the Rajah Arvo, of Dungally, met them as they landed, and conducted them to a small shed erected for the occasion. Tuan Hadjee there dressed the young man in a long pair of silk trowsers, and put on him five silk gowns of different colours, a small silk cap, and over that a turban; to complete the dress, he put a wrapper over all.

"Being now accoutred, he was placed on the outside of the shed; the Rajah of Dungally was stationed next to him, then Tuan Hadjee, and next to him the chief men of the prow. About twenty of the crew were picked out to walk before the bridegroom, all armed with spears and shields. They then proceeded from the beach to the town, which was no great distance. At the same time about thirty men, armed with spears and shields, came from the town as if to oppose them, when a sham fight was entered into, which they performed very well, gradually retreating towards the town as the bridegroom and his party advanced thereto. A *patempore*, or piece of chintz, was extended across the gateway, as if to prevent their entrance, till the Rajah's son had made a present to the men of Dungally; he therefore gave them some betel-nut and some serric, which they chew with the betel, on which they withdrew the *patempore*. He then advanced about two rods farther, when the *patempore* was again put across, at the same time his people and those of the opposite party appeared to shew the greatest anger towards each other, by darting spears over each other's heads until another present was made. The *patempore* was again removed, and replaced as before at short distances, till he reached the house where the bride was. He then went up, ascended the steps to go into the house, at the door of which the *patempore* was again placed, where he was required to make a larger present. He took out of his pocket a handful of betel-nut and serric to give them, and, as they were reaching for it, they let the *patempore* slip, when he went past without giving them any, which caused considerable laughter, and the spectators gave a great shout. The bridegroom was then conducted into a large room where the bride was waiting to receive him, and he seated himself by her side.

The house was then crowded by all the great men of the place. Tuan Hadjee, who had followed the procession, now entered, and placed himself at the end of the room opposite to the bridegroom, to perform the marriage ceremony. He first married the bridegroom to the bride, by telling him that he must provide a house, servants, &c. for her; he then married her to him, exhorting her to forsake all other men, to be attentive to him, and to acknowledge him her superior. This ended, they made a *salam*, or thanksgiving. Tuan Hadjee then sang to a tune which was musical, lively, and pleasing, and used only on such occasions; at the close of it he was accompanied by all the guests. This being finished, supper was brought in. The bride and bridegroom then, for the first time, ate out of the same dish, and the rest of the company as they could, three or four together. After supper, the couple was conveyed to their apartment, which was richly hung with *patempores*. One or two bamboos of water was brought to them, and for seven days they were not seen in public, during which time water was carried to them night and morning, and provisions in abundance."

In the Island of CELEBES, when a man wishes

to take a wife, he must apply to the head Rajah, who summonses a meeting of the principal persons to examine the parents of either party, and know if they be agreeable. Polygamy is general, and a man is allowed to take as many wives as he can maintain; but is obliged to take a house for each of them. The first wife is always looked upon as the superior.

In MADAGASCAR, a woman who is repudiated by her husband is not at liberty to marry again till she has paid her late husband the sum he gave for her previous to their marriage.

In JAPAN, the marriage ceremony is performed before an altar, on an elevated situation near the town, by the bride lighting a torch, from which the bridegroom kindles another. Though polygamy be allowed, yet only one is acknowledged as the wife, the others being considered as concubines. Marriages are conducted by the parents or relations. The wife is under the absolute disposal of her husband, the law allowing no claim whatever, in case she incur his displeasure. Hence, though the women are not confined, infidelity is very rare. In case of separation, the wife is condemned to the ignominy of having her head always shaved.

AFRICA.

MOROCCO, ALGIERS, EGYPT, ABYSSINIA.

THE inhabitants of the kingdom of Morocco are so extremely jealous of any intercourse with Christians, that it is with the utmost difficulty any information respecting their amatory rites and customs can be obtained, as they do not suffer a Christian to be present at their marriage ceremonies. Polygamy and concubinage, however, as in all southern climates, is allowed and encouraged, and it is carried to such an extent in this country, that it is said that the Emperor Bensar had eight thousand wives and concubines; and it is no uncommon circumstance for Princes to have four or five thousand at one time. According to the Moresc laws, there are no bastards except the offspring of prostitutes.

M. Lempriere was allowed to see more of their amatory customs, perhaps, than any Christian who ever visited this country, who, being a surgeon, was admitted into the harem to prescribe for some of the ladies who were indisposed, and was by that means enabled to describe the interior of this female prison, and, what is still more curious, the manners and behaviour of its inhabitants. The harem forms a part of the palace; the apartments, which are all on the ground floor, are square, very lofty, and four of them inclose a spacious square court, into which they open by means of large folding doors. In the centre of the courts, which are floored with blue and white chequered tiling, is a fountain, supplied by pipes from a large reservoir outside of the palace, which serves for the frequent ablutions of the Mahometan religion, as well as for other purposes. The whole of the harem consists of about twelve of those square courts, communicating with each other by means of several narrow passages, which afford a free access from one part of the palace to another, and of which all the women are allowed to avail themselves. The apartments are ornamented on the outside with beautiful carved wood. In the inside most of the rooms are hung with rich damask, of the most beautiful and various colours; the floors are laid with the most elegant carpets, having mattresses at different distances from each other for sitting or sleeping. Besides these, the apartments are furnished at each extremity with an elegant European mahogany bedstead, hung with damask, having on it several mattresses placed one over the other, which are covered with various coloured silks; but those beds are only put to ornament the room. In all the apartments, without exception, the ceiling is of wood, carved and painted. The principal ornaments of some were large and valuable looking-glasses, hung against various parts of the walls; in others, clocks and watches of different sizes, in glass cases, were disposed in the same manner.

The Sultana *Lalla Batoom* and another favourite were indulged with a whole square to themselves, but the concubines were only allowed a single room each. Every one had a separate daily allowance from the Emperor, in proportion to the estimation in which they were held by him. The late Emperor's allowance was very trifling. Lilla Douya, a favourite Sultana, had very little more than half-a-crown English a day, and the others less in proportion; though it must be allowed that the Emperor frequently made them presents in money, trinkets, and dress; but this could never be sufficient to support the number of domestics and other expences they must necessarily incur; their greatest dependence, therefore, was on the presents they received from those Europeans and Moors who visited the court, and who employed their influence to obtain some particular favour from the Emperor, which was the most successful mode that could be adopted. When M. Lemprier was at Morocco, a Jew, desirous of obtaining a very advantageous favour of the Emperor, for which he had long unsuccessfully applied, sent to all the principal ladies of the harem presents of pearls to a very large amount; the consequence was, they all went in a body to the Emperor, and obtained the wished-for concession.

The ladies separately furnish their own rooms, hire their own domestics, and, in fact, do what they please in the harem, but are not permitted to go out without an express order from the Emperor, who very seldom grants that favour, except when they are to be removed from one palace to another; in which case, a party of soldiers are dispatched a short distance before them, to disperse the male passengers in particular, and prevent their seeing of them. This previous step being taken, a piece of linen cloth is tied round the lower part of their face, after which those miserable females cover themselves all over with their haicks, and either mount mules, which they ride like men, or, as is more usual, they are put into a square carriage or litter, constructed for the purpose, having lattice-work, which allows of their seeing without being seen. In this manner they travel, under the charge of a guard of black eunuchs.

This journey, and sometimes a walk within the bounds of the palace, but with which they are seldom indulged, is the only exercise they are permitted to take. The late Emperor's harem consisted of from sixty to one hundred females, besides the domestics and slaves, which are very numerous. Many of the concubines were Moorish women who had been presented to the Emperor, as the Moors consider it an honour to have their daughters in the harem. There are several European slaves, who had either been purchased or taken captives, and also several negroes. In this groupe, the Europeans or their descendants have by far the greatest claim to the character of handsome. There was one in particular, a native of Spain, and taken into the harem about the same time as *Lalla Douya*, who was indeed a perfect beauty; nor was this lady singular in that respect, there being several others almost equally handsome. The eunuchs, who have the entire charge of the women, and who in fact live always among them, are the children of negro-slaves. They are generally either very short and fat, or else very tall, deformed, and lame. Their voices have that peculiar tone which is observable in youths just arriving at manhood, and their persons altogether afford a distinct image of weakness and effeminacy.

The same gentleman gives us a very curious account of the manners and ignorance of these immured females, from his own observations when visiting the harem of the prince. He relates that, being attended by a eunuch, "after passing the gate of the harem, which is always kept locked, and under the care of a guard of eunuchs, we entered a narrow and dark passage, which brought us to the court into which the women's chambers open. We here saw a great number of black and white women and children; some of them were concubines, some were slaves, and others hired domestics. Upon their observing the unusual figure of a European, the whole multitude in a body surrounded me, expressing the utmost astonishment at my dress and appearance. Some stood motionless in the usual attitudes of wonder and surprise, with their hands lifted up, their eyes fixed, and their mouths extended; others burst into immoderate fits of laughter; while again others came up close, and viewed me with uncommon attention from head to foot. The parts of my dress which seemed most to attract their notice were my buckles, buttons, and stockings, neither men nor women in this country wearing any thing of the kind. With respect to the club of my hair, they seemed utterly at a loss in what way to consider it; but the powder which I wore they conceived to be employed for the purpose of destroying vermin.

" Most of the children, when they saw me, ran away in the most perfect consternation; and, on the whole, I appeared as singular an animal, and I dare say had the honour of exciting as much curiosity and attention, as a lion or man-tiger just imported from abroad, and introduced into a country town in England on a market-day. Every time I visited the harem I was surrounded and laughed at by this curious mob, who, on my entering the gate, followed me close to the very chamber to which I was proceeding, and on my return universally escorted me out. The greater part of the women were uncommonly fat and unwieldly, had very black and full eyes, with round faces, and small noses. They were of various complexions; some very fair, some sallow, and others were perfect negroes. One of my new patients being ready to receive me, I was desired to walk into the room, where, to my great surprise, I saw nothing but a curtain drawn quite across the apartment, similar to that of a theatre which separates the stage from the audience. A female domestic brought me a very low stool, placed it near the curtain, and told me I was to sit down there and feel her mistress's pulse. The lady, who had by this time summoned up courage to speak, introduced her hand from the bottom of the curtain, and desired me to inform her of all her complaints, which she conceived I might perfectly do by merely feeling her pulse. It was in vain to ask her where the pain was seated; whether in her stomach, head, or back; the only answer I could rocure was a request to feel the pulse of her other hand, and then point out the seat of the disease, and the nature of the pain.

"Having neither satisfied my curiosity by exhibiting her face, nor made me acquainted with the nature of the complaint, I was under the necessity of informing her, in positive terms, that to understand the disease it was absolutely necessary to see the tongue as well as feel the pulse, without which I could do nothing for her. My eloquence, or rather that of my Jewish interpreter, was, however, for a long time exerted in vain: and I am persuaded she would have dismissed me without any farther enquiry, had not her invention supplied her with a happy expedient to remove her embarrasment. She contrived at last to cut a hole through the curtain, through which she extruded her tongue, and thus complied with my injunction as far as was necessary in a medical point of view, but most effectually disappointed my curiosity. I was afterwards ordered to look at another of the Prince's wives, who was affected with a scrophulous swelling in her neck. The lady was in the same manner as the other excluded from my sight; but she was obliged to show me her complaint, by which means I had an opportunity of seeing her face, which I observed to be very handsome."

It is curious to observe the simple and childish notions of persons excluded from the world. All the ladies of the harem expected that our author should instantly discover their complaints upon feeling their pulse, and that he could cure every one instantly. He found them proud and vain of their persons, and extremely ignorant. Among other ridiculous questions, they asked M. Lempriere's interpreter if M. Lempriere could read and write; being answered in the affirmitive, they were extremely surprised at the learning of the Christians. It is melancholy to reflect on the condition of these unfortunate women. Being considered as the mere instruments of pleasure, no attention is paid to the improvement of their minds. They have no employment to occupy their time. Their needlework is chiefly done by Jewesses; their food is dressed, and their chamber taken care of, by slaves and domestics. They have no amusement but a rude and melancholy kind of music, without melody, variety, or taste, and conversation with one another, which must indeed be very confined, uniform, and inanimate, as they never see a new object. Excluded from the enjoyment of fresh air and exercise, so necessary for the support of health and life; deprived of all society but that of their fellow-sufferers, a society to which most of them would prefer even solitude itself; they can only be considered as the most abject of slaves—slaves to the vices and caprice of a most licentious tyrant, who exacts, even from his wives themselves, a degree of submission and respect which borders upon idolatry, and which God and nature never meant should be paid to a mortal.

ALGIERS.—Among the Algerines, when a young man is inclined to marry, he drives a number of cattle to the tent where the lady resides. The girl and her parents generally consent on viewing the stock. All the young women of the *horde* are then invited to the feast. The bride is placed on a horse belonging to the bridegroom, and led home amidst the acclamations of all present.

On arriving at the bridegroom's door, a stick is given her, which she thrusts into the ground, and repeats the following line:—

As this stick is fasten'd in the ground,
So to my husband I'm in duty bound;
As violence alone can this remove,
So nought but death shall force me from his love.

She then alights, and, to show her willingness to do any duty her husband may assign her, she drives his flocks to water and back again. These previous ceremonies being settled, all the company enter the hut, and conclude the evening as festively as they can afford.

After the marriage the wife is obliged to wear a veil, never stirs from the hut a whole month, and ever after is excluded from all knowledge and participation in public affairs.

Among the higher orders polygamy is allowed, and marriage contracts are left to the interference of friends. When the union is agreed upon, the bridegroom sends a present to the bride, and invites her relations to a feast and musical entertainment, and the marriage ceremony is concluded with another feast and entertainment.

There is a law enacted here which is strictly put in execution. When a woman is guilty of fornication with a Christian, her head is tied in a sack, and she is thrown into the sea, unless the man agrees to turn Mahometan. Such examples are frequently seen, and yet both married women and single are continually intriguing with the Christians. The little affection they bear their husbands, and the restraint they labour under, are great inducements to their breaking the marriage vow.

Being confined to their houses, those who are married to Corsairs are continually inventing methods of injuring their husbands, which is put in practice during the long voyages he often makes. When the Corsair is at sea his wife is kept in the city, but on his return she is taken by him to his country house, where he unbends after his toils at sea.

Artifice and love have invented a method of intrigue unknown in any other country. A slave who is in love with and beloved by his mistress explains the several impulses of his passion by the manner in which he disposes a parterre. A nosegay, made in a certain manner, contains as many tender and passionate ideas as a letter of several pages. The flower-gentle, placed by a violet, shows that the lover hopes, when the husband is gone to sea, to meet such a return to his passion as will fully compensate for the evils his presence occasions. The orange-flower denotes hope; the marigold, despair; the amaranth, constancy; the tulip reproaches with being unfaithful; the rose is an encomium of beauty, &c. &c. by which means a tolerable language is formed. For instance, if a lover wants to inform his mistress he is driven to despair of the husband going, in this case he forms a nosegay of a marigold, an orange-flower, a violet, and a flower-gentle; these *billet-doux* are easily conveyed to the mistress, who returns her answer by the same method. They are always careful to communicate to each other their own method of arranging the flowers, that no other person may know the meaning but themselves, by which means they can sometimes converse even in the presence of their husbands.

EGYPT.—The marriages in Egypt are not, as in Europe, permanent contracts. If a man be desirous of parting from his wife, he goes before the judge, declares in his presence that he puts her from him, and when the four months' probation, enjoined by the law, are expired, he returns the wealth she brought, and the portion stipulated in the marriage contract. If they have children, the husband retains the boys, and the wife the girls; they are then free, and may marry elsewhere.

Contracts are made for the young men by their relations, as they meet most of the young women of the city at the baths, whom they perfectly describe, and the choice being made, the alliance is made mention to the father of the female, the portion specified, and if he consent they make him presents. The following day, the same persons go to the house of the bride, and tear her, as it were, violently away from the arms of her mother; she is then triumphantly conveyed to the house of the bridegroom.

The procession usually begins in the evening; dancers go before, and (if a person of rank) numerous slaves display the effects destined to the bride's use; numbers of dancing girls keep time with their instruments, and the young bride appears under a magnificent canopy, borne by four slaves, and entirely covered by a veil, embroidered with gold, pearls, and diamonds. A long file of flambeaux illuminate the procession, and the Almehs, in chorus, occasionally sing verses in praise of the bride and bridegroom. On their arrival at the house of the bridegroom, the men and women repair to separate apartments, those of the women being so constructed that they can see what is performing in the men's. The Almehs descend and display their ability and address in dances and pantomimical representations suitable to the occasion; this ended, they chaunt, in chorus, the epithalamium, extolling the allurements of the bride, and the bliss of that mortal who shall enjoy so many charms. During the ceremony, she passes several times before the bridegroom to display her wealth and elegance. The guests having retired, the husband enters the nuptial chamber, the veil is removed, and, for the first time, he beholds his wife. The inferor classes observe the same ceremonies, except that the procession is not so pompous.

The COPTS have a custom of betrothing girls at six or seven years of age, which is done by putting a ring on their finger; but permission is after obtained for her friends to educate her till she arrives at years of discretion. The Mahometans consider marriage as a civil institution, entirely detached from religion.

Among the ancient Egyptians, parents who killed their children did not suffer death, but were adjudged to embrace their dead bodies for three days; and guards were placed over them to see that they duly performed the sentence passed on them. Pregnant women were not executed till they were delivered. Parricides were punished with the most cruel and lingering death they could inflict.

At Bornou, in the vicinity of the great Desart of Zahara, when a young man is inclined to marry, he makes presents to the father of the girl whom he wishes to have, but he will not give up his daughter until he thinks a sufficient compensation has been paid for her; nor can the most pressing entreaties of the young people make him alter this resolution: and thus he who has most daughters is accounted the richest man. When they are united, if the man do not like his partner, he may send her back to her parents; but he cannot claim a return of his presents. He cannot, however, send her home without first obtaining the consent of the *horde*, which is merely nominal, it being never refused. The women are treated with the most sovereign contempt, never taking the name of their husbands.

Although the women are used so badly, and are very indecent in their gestures, yet they are generally faithful to their husbands. Instances of infidelity seldom occur; but when it does she is driven from the dwelling of her lord, and his relations mostly avenge the indignity done their family with her blood. They consider females as an inferior race of beings. Their ideas of beauty consist in excessive corpulence. The women never eat with their husbands; but, when they have prepared dinner, retire, and wait till he has dined; they then come in and partake of what is left. The girls, to make them fat, are compelled every morning to eat a large quantity of *cuscus*, and drink several jugs of camel's milk. Boys are generally taught to read and write Arabic; and as soon as they begin to grow up are respected by the women, and even their own mothers do not eat with them.

ABYSSINIA.—There is no form of marriage among the Abyssinians, except mutual agreement may be so termed, which is dissoluble at pleasure. They cohabit together when they please, and annul or renew the contract in the same manner. Thus a woman or man of the first quality may be in company with a dozen who have been their bridegroom or bride, though perhaps none of them may be so at present. Upon separation they divide the children. The eldest son falls to the mother's first choice, and the eldest daughter to the father; if there is but one daughter, and all the rest sons, she is assigned to the father; if but one son, and all the rest are daughters, he is assigned to the mother: should the numbers be unequal after the first election, the rest are divided by lot. There is no distinction from the prince to the beggar, of illegitimate or legitimate children.

The king in his marriage uses no other ceremony than this. He sends an Azage to the house where the lady resides; the officer announces to her it is the king's pleasure she should remove immediately to the palace. She then dresses herself in the best manner, and without any reluctance obeys. An apartment is assigned her in the palace, and a house given her where she chooses. When the king makes her what they call *Tteghe*, it has some faint resemblance of marriage; for, whether he be in the court or camp, he orders one of his officers to pronounce in his presence that he, the king, has chosen his handmaid, naming her, for his queen. A crown is then put upon her head, but she is not anointed.

The Jesuit Alvarez, who was present at a ceremony where the patriarch officiated, says, the bride and bridegroom were waiting at the church door, where a couch was prepared for them; and on which the patriarch ordered them to sit; he then, with a cross in one hand and a censor in the other, made a kind of procession round them; then, laying his hands on their heads, told them, as they had become one flesh, so they ought to have but one heart and mind. He then went into the church and performed divine service, when, giving them his blessing, the ceremony was ended. The more religious receive the holy communion. After consummation, the husband and wife keep separate tables; or, if they agree to eat together, bring their victuals ready dressed, or send it in by their slaves or attendants.

In the more civilized parts of Abyssinia all their marriages must be confirmed before a priest. They are given to polygamy, though the laws of their church forbid it. The previous ceremonies only consist in each agreeing to live together as long as they like each other; they then proceed to the door of the church, where the priest performs the ceremony, and gives them his blessing. Divorces are very easily obtained; they then petition the priest for a permission to marry again, which is as easily obtained; though, in either case, the party may be excluded the communion for a time at the discretion of the priest. In cases of infidelity, they compensate the injured party by presents; but, in case they cannot agree as to the compensation, the man is sentenced to pay a fine, which is appropriated to the use of the injured wife.

CAPE OF GOOD HOPE AND SIERRA LEONE.

HOTTENTOT marriages are made by the parents or nearest relations; and if the female disapprove of the match, she is nevertheless compelled to pass the night with the man whom her friends have chosen. If he force her to consummation, she is constrained to become his wife; but, on the contrary, if she preserve herself uncontaminated, she is ever after free from him. Should the nuptials take place, the day after an ox is killed to feast the company, who not only eat the flesh, but also besmear themselves with the blood and fat, powder themselves with a stuff they call *bucku*, and paint their cheeks with red chalk. The marriage ceremony is thus performed: The men squat in a circle, as, indeed, they do upon most occasions, and the bridegroom is placed in the centre; the women, also, in the same manner, form another circle to surround the bride. The priest then goes from one circle to the other, and alternately urines on the bride and bridegroom, who make furrows with their nails in the grease with which they are plastered, in order to rub in the precious libation; he then pronounces the nuptial benediction in the following words: "May you live happily together! may you have a son before a year is expired! may he be a good huntsman and a great warrior!" When they have dined, a pipe is filled with tobacco, which each successively smokes from, taking two or three whiffs, when they hand it to their neighbour. It is singular, that, though the Hottentots are immoderately fond of spirituous liquors, music, and dancing, yet they use neither at their weddings. Polygamy is permitted, but the richest seldom have more than three wives. Marriage between first and second cousins is prohibited upon pain of death.

The portion they give a son on his marriage is usually two cows and two sheep; to a daughter, one of each, which are to be returned to the father if the bride die without having any children; but, if she ever bore any children to her husband, even though they are defunct, the portion becomes his. Divorces are permitted, if the party can show sufficient cause to the heads of the village; but adultery is punished with death. A man who has been divorced may marry again, but a woman may not, while her former husband is living.

When a widow is inclined to enter again into the married state, she must give a severe proof of her inclination thereto, being under a necessity of losing a joint of her little finger, which is repeated every time she is married after the first. A new-born child, after having its nose flattened, is always rubbed over first with fresh cow-dung, then with a juice expressed from the stalks of the African fig; thirdly, with sheep's fat or melted butter, and lastly, well powered with *bucku*. Male twins occasion great joy to the parents; if female twins, they destroy the least favoured; if one is male, the other female, they inevitably destroy the latter. When a child is still-born, they deem it a bad omen, and immediately remove their hut.

When the child has been smeared, greased,

and daubed, as above, the mother gives it what name she thinks proper, which is usually that of some wild or tame animal. When the woman is well again, she then daubs herself with cow-dung, which they look upon as a kind of purification. Being thus delightfully perfumed, and elegantly decorated with sheep's guts, she is permitted to go abroad or see company.

The eldest son has encouragement to exercise a kind of tyranny over his brothers and sisters. The male Hottentot is deemed of age at eighteen, when he is admitted into society, at which time a feast is given, but the youth himself is not permitted to partake thereof, until all who are present have been served. It is then expected that he should behave ill to women in general, and to his mother in particular, in order to evince his contempt for every thing which is feminine. Indeed it is usual for a youth when admitted into male society to go home and cudgel his mother; nor does she disapprove thereof, but congratulates herself for having had the happiness to bring so spirited a youth into the world: so much does custom reconcile us even to things which are in themselves unnatural.

A Hottentot never is permitted to have cattle

or a hut until he is married, after his eighteenth year living under the inspection of his father, as before that period he was under the direction of his mother. As soon as he is married, his wife becomes his slave; she does all the drudgery, and has all the care of domestic concerns on her, the husband giving himself totally up to inaction and idleness.

Among the slaves at the Cape of Good Hope, under the Dutch government, there was not any form of marriage. No long services engage the affections; no priest bestows his benediction on the nuptial bed; no parent gives away his daughter, and assembles his friends on the happy day;—slavery lights the marriage torch—slavery leads them, alone and unattended, to the marriage-bed. The husband visits his wife as he can find opportunities, and leaves her when he pleases to take another, without ceremony, without reproach.

In SIERRA LEONE, polygamy is practised. The women are frequently hostages for alliance and peace. The chiefs, who have been at war, cement their treaties by an exchange of their daughters; private individuals do the same; and this may account why the chiefs have such numbers of women. A girl is frequently betrothed to a man as soon as she is born, and on the day agreed on for the marriage the bridegroom places on the road which the bride has to pass several persons with brandy and other refreshments; for, if these articles be not furnished, the conductors of the bride will not advance a step further, though they may have got three parts on their journey. On approaching the town, they stop, till joined by the friends of the bridegroom, who testify their joy by shouting, drinking, and firing their guns. At this period an old woman takes the girl upon her shoulders, and the attendants cover her with a fine veil, for from that moment no man must see her face till the consummation of the marriage. Mats are spread before the old woman, who carries her, as she must not touch the ground with her feet. In this manner the bride is conveyed to the house of her husband, followed by the friends of both families, singing, dancing, and firing off their musquets. Towards evening the husband comes into the apartment of his wife. If he have reason to suspect her chastity, he immediately leaves the room, which is no sooner known among the friends, than those who have conducted her to him hasten from the sight of observers, crying and howling with shame and confusion; if, on the other hand, he is satisfied, he remains with her the whole night, the friends rejoice, and next day the testimonials of her virginity are carried through the streets in triumph. In both cases, however, the husband may keep the girl; but, should he send her back, he must return all that she has brought him.

From these details it will be seen that chastity is a virtue highly esteemed among the Africans, at least till marriage; but from that moment it is a trait of unpoliteness and want of education in a woman to resist the importunities of a lover; she would indeed be punished if discovered, but her reputation would remain unsullied. Among the black savages of Africa we find the customs which are prevalent in Italy and Spain, for each negro lady has a Cicisbeo or Cortejo, whom she makes choice of and consults on all occasions. The husband is obliged to tolerate this intercourse in silence; nevertheless, there are laws sufficiently severe to punish adulterers, but they are of little effect, unless they are applied to by a man of great power; and even then he dare not make a great bustle, on account of the ridicule to which he would be exposed. It is mostly among the great men that the above is practised, who keep a number of women.

A remarkable and truly extraordinary circumstance is, that the women never impose illegitimate children on their husbands, always declaring before accouchement who is the father. If, however, the husband wishes to have a child of his own by a woman he loves, he obliges her to swear she will be true to him for a certain time; she takes the oath, and generally keeps it; but if in the interval, either by violence or the persuasion of her lover, she breaks her promise, she confesses her fault immediately to her husband, which is the more singular, as they are ever after devoted to shame and infamy.

The union of a white man with a black or a mulatto is not indissoluble, but only lasts during the pleasure of the parties, nor does a separation reflect any discredit.

A black woman in general thinks herself honoured in partaking of the touch of a white man, and is true, submissive, and grateful, to the utmost; in short, she uses every art to merit his kindness and love. If the husband embark to cross the sea, the disconsolate wife accompanies him to the shore, and sometimes follows him by swimming a considerable way after the vessel till her strength is exhausted; when obliged to return, she gathers up the sand on which are the last impressions of his footsteps, which she ties up in a piece of cotton, and lays under her pillow.

The women never wean their children till able to run alone: their husbands, during the time they are suckling, never cohabit with them, looking upon an infringement of this rule as a crime of the most heinous nature.

Many of the inhabitants of the banks of Sierra Leone perform that operation upon females which among the Turks is only practised upon the males; the ceremony of which operation is as follows:—Every year during the fine season, when there is a new moon, all the marriageable young girls in a village are assembled. The night preceding the day of the ceremony they are conducted by the women of the place to the most secret part of a wood, the avenues to which are scattered with amulets, the object of which is to keep away every person who is inclined to pry into their secrets, whose presence would profane the ceremony. The girls are there secluded for upwards of a month, during which period no human being, except the woman who performs the ceremony, is suffered to see them, and she every morning brings to them their food; if her decease or any other obstacle prevents her bringing them their supply of food, the woman who is to succeed her in this office, as she approaches the spot, calls with a loud voice to give notice of her approach, deposits the victuals at a certain place, and then hastens away without seeing any of them, or their seeing her; for, whether by chance or inclination, any one who violates this sanctuary is punished with death.

It is at this period only, when the body is reduced by the austerities they undergo in this place, and the mind prepared by the religious obscurity and silence of the forest in which they remain, that the girls are taught and initiated into the customs of the country, for till this period they are not esteemed worthy of knowing them. At length, when the time of their retreat expires, and the wound caused by the operation is nearly healed, they are taken back to the village with the same forms used as at leaving it; and, when arrived, they are received by all the women therein quite naked, and in this state they parade the streets with musical instruments by day-light. Their return from the wood is succeeded by a month's probation, during which time they are each day conducted in procession, accompanied by music, and covered from head to foot, to the houses of the principal inhabitants, where they sing and dance till the owner makes each of them a present. When the month is expired, they are liberated from all those ceremonies, and given to the men intended for their husbands.

Neither the origin nor the motives of this ceremony is known; but, so great is their veneration for it, that the most shocking of all insults is to reproach them with not having done it honour; and this reproach is even lavished on strangers, who may not have come among them until after the time appointed for the rite.

COAST OF GUINEA, &c.

AMONG the inhabitants of WHYDAH, on the Gold Coast, there is the most unlimited indulgence given to polygamy, a poor man having frequently forty or fifty wives, and a prince sometimes four or five hundred, and a king as many thousands. These women, however, can only be considered as so many slaves, the chief part belonging to great people, being such captives as they choose rather to keep than sell to Europeans. Their marriage ceremonies are very trifling: when a man fancies a young woman, he applies to her father, and desires her for his wife, which is seldom refused;—he then presents the bride with a fine *pagne*, or garment, and with necklaces and bracelets; he then provides a grand entertainment, which concludes the ceremony. When a slave wishes to marry, he asks the consent of the girl's master, without applying to her parents: the children of this marriage belong to the master of the wife. Indeed, the women in general are little better than slaves. They till the ground, and do many other laborious kinds of work; nor are the favourite wives, who stay at home, by any means exempt from work, being always obliged to attend upon their husbands, and behave towards them with the greatest submission. It is little to be wondered at there being such great numbers of slaves, for, from the multiplicity of wives which every man has, a great number of children must reasonably be expected.

It is no uncommon thing for a father to have two hundred children living at the same time; and it often happens that a man has five or six born to him in one day. They never cohabit with their wives during pregnancy, which is the principal reason given for their taking so many. A man's principal wealth consists in the number of his children, all of whom he can dispose of at pleasure, except his eldest son.

On the death of the father of a family, the eldest son takes possession of every thing, not only of the goods and cattle, but also of his wives and children, which he immediately holds, and retains as his own, except his own mother, for whom, in case she desires it, he provides separate apartments and subsistence.

The punishment for adultery is no less severe than for murder, especially if committed with the wife of a prince or grandee. If the guilty party be surprised, the king immediately pronounces sentence of death, which is executed in the following manner:—They dig two graves, in one of which they plant a stake, and the woman is tied thereto; on the top of the other grave they lay iron bars, across which the man is fastened, and a fire kindled under; he is then literally roasted alive in the presence of the woman, and the punishment would be dreadfully lingering, were it not that they generally laid the criminal with the face downward. When the man is dead, they fling the body into the grave. After which there is a number of women, perhaps forty or fifty, come from the palace richly dressed, as if for a feast or merry-making; they are guarded by the king's musqueteers, each carries a pot of scalding water, which they pour upon the adultress, and also throw the pot on her head. This done, they loosen the body, take up the stake, and cast altogether into the grave.

When the wife of a grandee is guilty of adultery, he may either put her to death immediately, or sell her as a slave to the Europeans. If he determine on the former, the king is sufficiently satisfied with being made acquainted with the circumstance of the fact. The injured husband, however, has not the power of inflicting immediate punishment, unless he detect the guilty party in the fact. Otherwise he must bring them to trial, when they are usually punished with death.

The Chevalier Marchais, who was present at

one of these executions, gives the following account thereof:—

"A grandee complained to the king that a private person had debauched his wife; his Majesty, upon hearing the witnesses, sentenced the adulterer to be beaten to death wherever he could be found, and the body left there until it was devoured or rotten. The officers belonging to the Governor of *Sabi* found the culprit just entering his own door; they soon dispatched him with their clubs, and left the body as the king had ordered. The neighbours went to acquaint the captain of the seraglio that the body would infect all that quarter of the town where it lay before it was consumed, and entreated he would obtain the king's orders for its removal. The officer represented their complaint to the king, who replied, 'If I did not punish adultery with severity, no person in my country could be safe. The body shall lay there till it be devoured or rotten. The people shall see it, and learn at the expense of this wretch how they invade their neighbour's bed. All I grant is, that they may in the day-time throw a mat over the body, leaving the face uncovered, that all persons may see the countenance of him who has defiled his neighbour's wife, and detest him.' Not content with this, the king gave all the effects of the offender to the injured man."

The mother of the king of Whydah has more power, and is less under controul, than any other subject in his dominions, even superior to the queen herself; but she is under the necessity of continuing a widow the rest of her life. So jealous is the king of his wives, that, if a man should meet one of them in the street, and by the merest chance touch her, she would not be permitted to enter the *seraglio* again, and both she and the man would be sold for slaves. If it should appear there was any premeditation in their coming in contact, the woman would be sold, the man put to death, and all his effects confiscated to the king; for which reason, those, who have occasion to go to the palace, on their entrance call out *ago*, which signifies make way, or retire; the women then range themselves on one side, and the men pass on the other.

In like manner, when any of the king's wives go to work in the fields, whoever meets them must immediately fall on their knees, and remain in that position until they have passed. Although the people are obliged to pay such respect to them, the king himself shews them very little; they attend him on all occasions like servants, and, instead of shewing any affection for them, he treats them with the greatest disdain, haughtiness, and contempt.

As he considers them only in the light of slaves, so on the most trifling occasion he will sell them for slaves to the Europeans; and sometimes, when vessels are on the coast waiting to complete their cargo, he will supply them with whatever number they are in want of from his seraglio, which deficiencies are soon made up by the assiduity of his captains or governors of the seraglio, who go about the streets and seize such girls as they think will be pleasing to the king, nor dare any of his subjects make the least objection or resistance. The officers immediately present them to the king, and, as they are the handsomest girls they could meet with, his Majesty is sometimes particularly attracted by their beauty; when this happens to be the case, the object that most takes his fancy is honoured with his company for two or three nights, after which she is discarded, and must pass the remainder of her life in obscurity; for which reason the women are so little desirous of becoming the king's wife, that they would rather lead a life of celibacy.

Some of the inhabitants of GUINEA use the following marriage ceremonies. When a father finds his son able to get his own living, he looks out for a wife for him, unless the son may have provided himself. When they have agreed, the father communicates it to the parents of the young woman, who seldom dissent. A priest is then sent for, who, after administering the *fetish*, or oaths, in which the woman swears to love and be faithful to her husband, he also swears to love her, but omits the point of fidelity. When this ceremony is over, the parents make mutual presents, and the company spend the day in mirth and merriment. In the evening the husband sends his wife home, attended by her relations and friends, who stay a whole week with her, when they leave her, and she enters upon her ordinary employment.

These people dispose of their daughters when they are too young to consummate the marriage, in which case the ceremony is as follows:—On the day appointed for the wedding, all the kindred on both sides assemble at the house of the bride's father, where a great entertainment is prepared. In the evening the bride is taken to the bridegroom's house, and put into her husband's bed between two women; this ceremony is repeated three successive nights, after which she is sent back to her father's house, where she remains until of age to consummate the marriage. Some have twenty or thirty wives, as the more wives they have, the more they are respected; but common people seldom have more than ten. All their wives are employed in tilling the ground and managing the affairs of the family, except two, who (particularly if the husband be rich) are exempt from labour. The principal is called *Muliere Grande*, or the great wife; the second is called the *bossum*, because she is consecrated to their deity. Those two are generally the handsomest, on which account the husband is frequently jealous. He sleeps with them on fixed days, especially on their birth-day, and alternately every Tuesday, which is their fetish-day, or Sabbath. The easy situations of those wives make them sometimes much envied by the others, who are obliged to work hard, while the husband and his two wives are enjoying themselves without any labour. When the husband thinks proper to sleep with one of his other wives, he gives her a private intimation thereof, in order to prevent jealousy, and she retires to her apartment with the greatest privacy, and the matter is kept a profound secret.

The poor people of this country carry their children at their backs when at their labour, and, when they suckle them, raise the child to their shoulder, and turn the breast up to them. When they arrive at the age of ten or twelve, the father takes the boys under his care and instruction, and the mother keeps the girls.

The punishment for adultery is by fine, on which account many women, with consent of their husbands, bestow their favours so that the husband may take advantage of those who have thus injured them.* It is astonishing the subtleties they make use of to draw men into the snare, especially strangers; they will pretend that they have no husbands, and are yet free and unmarried; but the fact is no sooner over than they immediately disclose it to their husband. Others, whose admirers know them to be married, will swear eternal secrecy, but it is only with a design of drawing the lover in, for immediately they see their husband they will confess; indeed, the consequence might be fatal were they to conceal it, if the husband should come to the knowledge of it by any other means; but, by this method, they both gratify their own inclination and their husband's avarice.

The inland negroes are much more strict in cases of adultery than those on the coast. He who debauches a man's wife is not only ruined, but his relations often suffer with him; and if the injured party be rich, he will not only exact a fine, but very often the life of the offender. If the criminal be a slave, his life is inevitably forfeited, and a heavy fine laid on his master. A woman caught in adultery is also in great danger of losing her life, unless her relations can pacify her husband with money, or some valuable present; but her life is certainly forfeited if she be guilty with a slave of her husband's, and also the slave's, in a most cruel manner, in addition to which her relations are heavily fined; and, if adultery be committed with any of the king's wives, the man is buried alive, and the woman burnt.

The QUOJAS, of Guinea, allow polygamy as in most other countries, the first wife always having the pre-eminence. The husband takes care of and maintains the boys, the wife does the same by the girls. The ceremony of marriage consists chiefly of presents made by the parents of each party to the other; but the ceremony of naming the children is very particular. When a boy is to be named, the father walks through the village armed with bows and arrows; he keeps continually singing, and as he passes along the neighbours join him with musical instruments. As soon as the people are properly assembled, they form a ring, and the person appointed to perform the ceremony takes the child out of the mother's arms, lay it upon a shield, puts a bow into one hand, and a quiver into the other. He then makes a long harangue to the people, after which he addresses himself to the infant, wishing the child may be like its father, industrious, hospitable, and a good husbandman. He then names the child, after which the company retire; the men to hunt for game, which they bring to the hut of the child's parent, with palm wine, and the evening is concluded with festivity. They use the same ceremonies at the naming of a girl, only instead of a bow and arrow, they put a small shaft of wood into the child's hand, exhorting her to be a good housewife, dutiful to her husband, chaste, and affectionate, that he may love her above all his other wives: the day is then concluded as with naming a boy.

If a woman be accused of adultery, she is allowed to swear that she is innocent. Should it be afterwards proved that she has sworn falsely, she is publicly led by her husband to the market-place, where a council sit to hear the merits of the case. They first invoke the *Jannanin*, after which they cover the woman's eyes, that she may not see the spirits that they pretend to raise. She then receives a severe reprimand for the disorderly life she has led, with the most dreadful threats if she ever does the like again. A horrid noise then ensues, after which she is set at liberty by the *Jannanin*, upon promising to live more regularly in future. If, however, she should relapse again, the *bellino* and his attendants go early in the morning to the place where she resides, and with horrid noises seize and convey her to the market-place, where the council again sit, round which she must walk three times, that they may have an opportunity of viewing her; none but the brotherhood, or priests, who are to have the manegement of the trial must be present; any others must not even presume to look out of the windows. When the proceedings, which are kept entirely to themselves, are over, she is conducted to a sacred grove called *belli*, and is never after heard of. The negroes in general think they are carried away by the spirits, but it is most likely, and indeed some of the more sensible think the same, that they are put to death by the priests, but at the same time allege that it is done merely to pacify the *belli*, or god.

In some parts of the Gold Coast the wife who is first delivered of a boy is distinguished as the favourite, or chief; but this distinction is frequently fatal to her, for, if the husband die first, she must follow his corpse to the grave, and be buried alive with it. Monsieur Marchais, who was once an eye-witness to this dreadful ceremony, gives the following description of it:—

"The captain, (says he,) or chief of the village, dying of a hard drinking bout of brandy, the cries of his wives immediately spread the news through the village. All the women ran and howled like furies, the favourite wife distinguishing herself by her grief, and not without cause. However, as several women in the same case have prudently thought fit to make their escape, the rest of the women, under pretence of comforting her, took care she should have no opportunity of escaping. The relations of the deceased came to pay their respects to the body. When the *macabout* had examined the body, and ascertained that the death was natural, he, with his assistants, washed and dried the corpse, and then rubbed it all over with fat; they afterwards stretched it upon a mat in the middle of the house. The wives of the deceased went then round it, and his other women and relations next to them, the favourite being placed near the head, as the post of honour; several other women formed a circle round them, each of them endeavouring to outroar the others, tearing their hair, and scratching themselves methodically, like people who knew perfectly well the part they were to act. Sometimes they were silent for a while, while others repeated the actions and praises of the deceased, and then beginning their lamentations afresh. This mock music lasted two hours, when four lusty negroes entered the hut, and tied the dead body on a hand-barrow made of branches of trees; then, lifting it on their shoulders, they carried it through the town, running as fast as they could, and reeling about as if they were intoxicated, and making a thousand ridiculous gestures, very suitable to the lamentations making by the women who attended the procession. In short, the noise was as great as would have drowned the loudest thunder. This parade being over, the body was taken from the hand-barrow, and deposited on the ground; after which the extravagances of the women began afresh. During this the *marabut* made a deep grave, large enough to contain two bodies. He also killed and skinned a goat, the pluck of which served for a ragout, of which he, his assistants, and the favourite wife, ate some, but she seemed to have very little inclination thereto, knowing it was to be the last. She did eat some however, and during this time the body of the animal was divided into small pieces and broiled, of which the rest of the attendants partook. The lamentations began again, and, when the *marabut* thought it time to end the ceremony, he took the devoted wife by the arms, and delivered her to some stout negroes, who, seizing her roughly, tied her feet and hands behind her, and, laying her on her back, placed a piece of wood upon her breast, and, holding each other by the shoulders, they stamped upon the wood till they had broken her breast. Having thus at least half dispatched the unhappy victim, they tossed her into the grave with the remainder of the goat, throwing the body of her husband upon her, and immediately filling up the grave with stones, &c. The lamentations then ceased, and each returned home apparently as unconcerned as if nothing had happened.

In DAHAMOY, a country of Upper Guinea, the marriage ceremonies are very concise. When a man fancies a young woman, he applies to her father, and desires her for his wife, which is seldom refused. He then presents her with a fine pagne, or garment, necklaces, bracelets, &c.; he then provides a grand entertainment, which concludes the ceremony. Polygamy is universally prevalent. Their wives may be considered only as so many slaves, and indeed the principal part of those belonging to the great being chiefly captives they have taken a fancy to keep, instead of selling them for slaves. If a slave be inclined to marry another, he asks her master's permission: the boys of this marriage are the property of the wife's master.—Perhaps one reason of their being allowed to take so many wives is, that they never cohabit with a woman while she is pregnant. A man's chief wealth is his children, whom he can dispose of at pleasure, except his eldest son, who inherits all his father's wealth, even his wives, except his own mother, to whom, at his father's death, he provides a separate subsistence and apartment, if she desire it.

In the kingdom of BENIN polygamy is allowed in the same degree as on the Coast of Guinea, and their marriage ceremonies consist only in the consent of parents, a present to the bride, and an entertainment to the friends of either party. The men are exceedingly jealous, for which reason the wives of the poor enjoy a liberty to which those of the great are strangers; for, while the former have their liberty, the latter are closely confined, in order to obviate all possible means of intriguing. When a woman is delivered of a boy, it is presented to the king as his property; hence all the men in the kingdom are slaves to the king, but the girls are the property of their fathers. If a woman happen to have twins, information is sent to the king, who orders public rejoicings, it being considered as a happy omen, except at a place called *Arebo*, where they look upon such an event in so opposite a light, that they generally sacrifice both the woman and children to a certain demon which they suppose inhabits a wood near the town. Sometimes, indeed, they will spare the wife, upon the husband offering a female slave instead, but the children are condemned without redemption. Bosman says that, while he was at this town in 1699, he knew a merchant's wife thus redeemed, but her children were instantly sacrificed, whose fate she often deplored with tears. The following year he mentions the like having happened to the wife of a priest; she was delivered of two children, which, with a slave in the room of his wife, the priest, by virtue of his office, was under the necessity of sacrificing with his own hands. This shocking custom is still prevalent in that town, but of late years those who are able to defray the expense send their wives to be brought to bed in a more humane part of the country, by which means they avoid the necessity of the above cruel custom.

Adultery is punished variously, according to the circumstances of the parties. If a man detect his wife in the fact, he is entitled to all the effects of the offender, and the woman, after a severe drubbing, is discarded, and for the rest of her life must shift for herself. The better sort endeavour to bribe the injured husband, whose generosity is often thus induced to overlook the too great liberality of the inconstant spouse.

In CONGO, some who are converted to the Romish church are married according to the rites thereof; those who follow their ancient customs are thus married:—When a young man fancies a young woman, the parents of the former send a present to those of the latter, requesting the girl in marriage for their son; if her parents keep the presents, it is a token of compliance. The bridegroom then goes to the bride's residence, and brings her to his own, a priest is sent for, who binds the bargain, and the day is concluded with festivity and mirth. Should the husband have any reason to be displeased with his wife, he sends her again to her friends, and recovers his presents; but, should the blame rest with the husband, he cannot recover the presents. It is to be remarked that, when the friends of the girl receive the presents, they must not complain of their being small, be they ever so trifling, as that would be looked upon as wishing to sell her, to prevent which the extent of the presents is determined by their laws, according to circumstances. A man detected in adultery must give, as a compensation, a slave; the women receives no other punishment than merely asking her husband's pardon. Those detected in fornication are fined according to their circumstances.

The inhabitants of MUNDINGO, in Negroland, marry very young; some of them are contracted as soon as born, and the parent can never after annul the agreement; the man, however, when arrived at a proper age, if he please, can refuse to accept them; but the woman has not the power either of annulling the engagement, or of performing another. Before a man takes his wife, he must give her parents two hundred colas, (a fruit which grows in the inland parts of the country,) two iron bars, and a couple of cows. When a man takes home his wife, he makes a great entertainment, to which as many as please come without any invitation. The bride is brought on men's shoulders, with a veil over her face, which is not on any account to be removed until the marriage is consummated; till then the company amuse themselves with singing, dancing, buffoonery, &c.

Every man has the liberty of taking as many wives as he chooses, and, if he finds any of them false, of selling them for slaves. He likewise can, upon any occasion, put any one or more of his wives away, and make her take with her the whole of her children, or which of her children he does not choose to keep to himself, generally retaining those who are able to assist him in his employment; he may, even after parting from his wife, insist upon her returning to him, or, if he thinks any of the children which she took with her in the first instance will be serviceable to him, he can go and take them away from her. Wives pay such distinguished regard to their husbands, that, if they have been absent but a short time, the wife on his return salutes him on her knees; they also take the same position when presenting drink to their husband.

At BAMBARA, Mr. Park relates, that, while he was prisoner in a camp, he heard the sound of drums, and, upon enquiring the cause, he was informed that it was the celebration of a wedding among some of the neighbouring tents.

Shortly after an old woman entered his hut with a bowl in her hand, the contents of which she emptied on him. Mr. Park, finding that it was the same sort of holy water as that with which the priest among the Hottentots besprinkles a new-married couple, he began to suspect that the old lady was actuated by malice or mischief, but she gave him seriously to understand that it was *a nuptial benediction from the bride's own person*, and which, on such occasions, is always received by the young unmarried Moors as a mark of distinguished favour.

The inhabitants of BAMBOUK, a kingdom of Ethiopia, admit of polygamy, and take as many wives as they can keep. The person who courts a girl first solicits her consent, and then demands her of her parents, to whom he presents a few pounds of salt, a little gold, and sometimes an ox or a sheep. To the girl he makes a present of from two to four pieces of cotton cloth, a few pairs of morocco sandals or slippers, some glass ornaments, amber, coral, cloves, some Dutch coins, and one or two baskets of millet. For this price he may obtain the daughter of a chief, or even a king. Among the lower classes less valuable gifts are given. When the presents have been accepted, the parent of the young woman conduct her to the house of her future husband, attended by a numerous train of women, musicians, dancers, &c. who chaunt the virtue and beauty of the bride, and the power, riches, and generosity, of the bridegroom. On the bride's arrival at the door of the bridegroom's house, she takes off her slippers, and receives from her attendants a calabash of water; she knocks at the door, it is opened, and she finds her intended sitting in the midst of the elders of his family, and, approaching toward him, she prostrates herself, bathes his feet with the water in the calabash, and dries them with the lower part of her apparel. This act of submission is the only ceremony performed at marriages. The husband then installs his wife in a cottage on his land, which has been constructed for her use, and where she finds every thing for her individual comfort and subsistence. The first woman espoused is with more propriety his wife, and maintains a degree of superiority over the others. She resides in the same house with her husband, and eats with him, but not at the same table; takes care of his slippers, and is consulted and heard on all domestic affairs. The other women, though they are legitimately married, must observe a certain deference towards the former; they are never suffered to enter the house of their lord unless sent for, and are obliged to leave their slippers at the door; they are, in fact, a sort of legitimate concubines, whom the husband regularly visits, staying alternately a week with each. Every wife enjoys her own private property. As the first has great influence, the others are interested in courting her favour, which they emulate each other to obtain by making her presents.

The following is a marriage ceremony at Bird's Island, off Goree:—The bride, a beautiful black girl, had a profusion of ornaments about her, consisting of bracelets, rings, necklaces, a rich veil, &c. They had a drum beating, and were clapping of hands; the company formed a ring, in the midst of which two women by turns danced, and then joined the circle again. The next day they went in procession round the streets, which was continued for several days, the bride being supported by one of her friends, accompanied by dancing, singing, &c. and receiving refreshments at various places, and accompanied by the governor. If an officer or settler want a wife, he must court the girl for a month, and then give a dinner, keeping open house for several days, which sometimes costs two hundred pounds. Among the poorer classes, it is common for every one who goes to a wedding-dinner to give each a piece of money, as they can afford. Travellers bear testimony to the modest and orderly conduct of the black young women, though climate makes them go almost naked.

The inhabitants of the right bank of the SENEGAL are more solicitous to obtain corpulent women than graceful, and she that can move with the assistance of two men is but an indifferent beauty; while the lady who cannot stir, and is only to be moved on a camel, with long teeth projecting out of her mouth, is esteemed as a perfect paragon. To obtain this corpulence, mothers feed their daughters with a stuff called *cuscus*, which induces fat and unwieldiness, so necessary to obtain admirers. When a woman is brought to bed, if it be of a daughter, she blacks her face half over, in which state she suffers it to remain twenty days; but if she have a boy, she blacks her face all over, and lets its continue forty days, in which state they made a most dismal appearance.

The inhabitants of JEDDO punish adultery in the following manner:—The woman is close shaved, which they look upon as the greatest disgrace which can be inflicted upon a female; the man pays a fine, and upon failure thereof the injured party has a right to strip him quite naked wherever he finds him, and has also a right to demand assistance of any who are at hand.

Some of the African tribes have no form of marriage, merely purchasing the girl of her father for a few bottles of brandy, or at most a few clothes, upon payment of which, the father conducts his daughter to the hut of her husband, who immediately orders her to fetch water or some other domestic employment, that she may immediately be acquainted with her future occupations.

AMERICA.

SOUTH AMERICA.

AMONG the PERUVIANS, they celebrate marriage in the following singular manner. The Inca, in whose person was vested the highest dignities of the priest of the sun and king of men, convoked annually to Cusco all the marriageable young men and women of his family. The stated age for the former was twenty-four years, for the latter, eighteen. They were not permitted to marry earlier, as not being considered before that period capable of managing their families. The Inca being seated, the parties who had agreed to a union stood by each other, forming a circle round him. After calling them by name he joined their hands, and exacted a promise of mutual fidelity from them; he then delivered them to their parents. The celebration of the wedding was kept at the bridegroom's father's, and continued for two or three days. Such were the only marriages among that class deemed lawful.

The sons and daughters of citizens were married by priests, according to the division of the several districts in higher and lower Cusco.—The moveables and utensils of the houses of the new-married couple were supplied by their relations, every one bestowing according to his circumstances. The governors and *curacas* were obliged, by their offices, to marry after the same forms the young men and maidens of the provinces, &c. over which they preside; for, being considered as lords and fathers of the districts entrusted to their care, they were bound to assist in person to solemnize the marriages.

Marriages between persons in the first degree of consanguinity in the first line, or even in the collateral, was never permitted, except to the Incas, the legitimate heirs of the empire, and the sovereign alone espoused his own sister.—The vanity of those princes, who considered themselves little inferior to divinities, induced them to establish this law, to the exclusion of the rest of the family, that the race of the sun might be more pure in the blood of the monarch.

The Inca Garcillasso de la Vege affirms, that this ceremony is as ancient as the foundation of the Peruvian Monarchy, and that it was instituted by *Mango Capac*, the founder of the empire. Acosta, on the contrary, attributes it to one of their latest *Incas*, and with a zeal dictated by religious, but, perhaps, more by interested motives, in wishing to extenuate the cruelties inflicted by his countrymen on the innocent people, says, that it drew upon the royal family and upon the different branches of the empire, the wrath of heaven, which delivered them over a prey to the Spaniards, the instruments of its vengeance.

In MEXICO, marriages are celebrated by the authority of the priests; an instrument was drawn up, specifying the particulars of the wife's fortune, which, in case of separation, he must return; in which case the husband takes the boys, and the wife the girls, and after such separation they must not live together again on pain of death. When the articles of marriage were fully arranged, the parties went to the temple, where they communicated to the priest the particulars of their resolutions. He thereupon laid hold of a corner of her veil, and of the husband's mantle, and tied them together to indicate that they should remain inseparable. They afterwards approached a fire, which had been kindled for the occasion, and was considered the mediator of all family discontent. Having followed the priest seven times round the fire, they seated so as each should be equally warmed thereby, which they conceived to be the completion of matrimony. In the early part of the night, the bride, conducted by several of her own sex, each with a torch in her hand, went to the bridegroom's abode, where a marriage festival was prepared.

Among the inhabitants of NICARAGUA, the priest, in performing the ceremony of marriage, takes the parties by the little finger, and leads them to a fire kindled for the occasion; he there instructs them in their duty, and in such particular conduct as he may judge requisite for them to be informed of in the state they are about to enter upon. When the fire is burnt out, the parties are looked upon as legally married.

The THASCALANS used to shave the heads of the new-married couple, to denote that all useful sports should in the married state be abandoned.

In one province of the Mexican empire, it was customary to carry the bridegroom to be married, that it might seem as if against his consent.

In the province of PANUCO, a husband purchased his wife, and her father did not speak to his son-in-law for the first year of his marriage. The husband and wife did not cohabit for two years after the birth of the first child. The Macatecas, another province of Mexico, fasted, prayed, and sacrificed to their gods for twenty days after marriage, and likewise drew from themselves blood, with which they sprinkled their idols. The mutual consent of the parties was all that was requisite for a separation; but they were on pain of death prohibited from a re-union; a statute, whose penalties were so severe, rendered divorces unfrequent. Female chastity was held in high estimation, and a breach of conjugal fidelity was regarded as highly criminal.

In NEW GRENADA, where polygamy is allowed, the ties of consanguinity are respected. The Cacique has usually a greater number of wives than any other of the people; and his successors are chosen from among the children of her to whom he was most attached.

The CARIBANIANS allowed the practice of

polygamy to its fullest extent, and a *cacique* frequently distributed his wives into different parts of the country. Feasting and dancing were introduced at the marriage ceremony, and the hair of the parties was cut off. The bride was obliged to pass the first night with the priest, as a form essentially necessary to constitute the legality of the marriage, which part being omitted, she was only considered as a concubine. Among the natives of America, it does not appear customary for a father to bestow any portion with his daughter. The practice of receiving a dower with a wife, which is not always productive of felicity in wedlock, prevails only in a degree as society has made advances in civilization, the arts, and a taste for luxury.

The custom of espousing a plurality of wives prevails among the natives of DARIEN; and the husbands have the privilege of selling their partners whenever they cease to be agreeable. Prostitution before marriage is said to be frequent, but as pregnancy is looked upon as ignominious then, they take every method of prevention. Attachment to each other from mutual affection is not necessary for forming engagements between the sexes; their gallantry extends no farther than to a proposal of marriage from the man, or the woman, it not being considered a mark of forwardness for the latter openly to declare her inclination. A present is brought to the door of the cabin of the bridegroom, by each guest invited to the marriage. The parties are conducted by their fathers into the cabin, the father of the bridegroom commencing the ceremony by an oration. He holds in his hands a bow, and arrows with the points directed towards the young couple; he dances until he becomes heated and fatigued, and afterwards kneeling down, he presents his son to the bride, whose father also performs the same gestures which the other exhibited. When the ceremony is concluded, a party of men begin to cut down trees and clear a spot of ground, on which they plant Indian corn for the future support of the young couple.

The young women among the CHAWANONS, who have any pretensions to beauty, practise a peculiar kind of coquetry. As soon as they arrive at the age of puberty, which commonly happens before they are twelve years of age, they either keep themselves quite excluded at home, or muffle themselves up so that when they go abroad it is impossible to see any thing but their eyes. On these indications of beauty they are eagerly sought in marriage, and those men who have the greatest reputation as warriors or hunters, generally obtain the consent of her family. After this the lover repairs to his cabin, where the beauty is lying closely enveloped on her couch; he gently approaches and uncovers her face, so that she may see his person, which if it be to her mind, she gives a smile of approbation that invites the youth to lie down by her side; should his person not please her, she again conceals her face more closely than before. The lover instantly retires, and no longer thinks of gratifying his passion, which among this people is only approved when reciprocally felt.—When the nuptial ceremony is ended, the new son-in-law is admitted into the cabin of his wife's father, but he must engage in the chase for the benefit of his father-in-law till the birth of his first child. He has the power of marrying all his wife's sisters as they arrive at puberty, or disposing of them to whom he pleases. The young savage seldom lives long with his first wife. Often before he is thirty or thirty-five, he has married and abandoned a dozen.

Among the CHACONESE, it was common for the females to propose matches as well as the men. With the *caciques*, or chiefs, it was lawful to marry the widow of a deceased brother, but it seldom was carried into practice; the Indians not approving of matches between relations, and ever since the introduction of Christianity they do not often marry within the degrees allowed by Christians. The women prick their faces, necks, and breasts, in order to mark them with a certain dye which they use as an ornament; they are very jealous of their husbands, but entertain little affection for their offspring. The husband, when his wife is brought to bed, observes a most rigorous fast, during which fast they neither hunted nor conversed with any one, it being their firm belief that the life of the child depends on their strict performance thereof. The ceremony they observed in giving names to their children was as follows:—A prisoner of war was plentifully entertained for several days previous to the naming of their children; on the appointed day his throat was cut; as soon as he was dead, all who were present touched the body, during which time they gave names to such children as had not received any. This done, the body was cut up, every family taking a piece thereof, which they boiled, and each person of a family taking some of the liquor, not excepting children at the breast.

In CALIFORNIA, the men have sacrificed much more to Christianity than the women. Peyrouse informs us they were formerly given to polygamy, and were even in the habit of espousing all the sisters of a family. The women, on the other hand, have acquired the privilege of receiving the caresses of one man. Some confess, however, that notwithstanding the unanimous report of the missionaries on polygamy, it cannot be conceived that it could be an established custom of a savage nation; for the number of men there being pretty nearly equal to the women, a forced continence must have been the consequence to many, unless that conjugal fidelity had been less rigorously observed there than in the missions where the religious have constituted themselves the guardians of the women's virtue. An hour after supper they have the care of shutting up, under lock and key, all those whose husbands are absent, as well as the young girls above nine years of age, and during the day they are instructed to the care af matrons. So many precautions are still insufficient; and we see men in the stocks, and women in irons, for having deceived the vigilance of these female Argusses.

The women mourn six months for the death of their husband, after which period they are permitted to marry again. The crime of adultery is punished with death in this country.

The ABISSANS sometimes practise polygamy, but not in general. The women often kill their children, that their whole attention may be bestowed upon their husbands. They marry at the age of from twenty to twenty-five. The girls are bought of their parents for about four horses. Their clothes are of various colours.

The OTTOMAQUES are the only Indians who admit their women to participate in their amusements. Among them, or elsewhere, the whole weigh of domestic labour falls upon the female; but they are at least allowed to associate in their public diversions. They are, beside, the only tribe among whom the practice of polygamy is not admitted. A singular custom also prevails with them, of always uniting a young man to an old woman, or a young woman to an old man,

The reason they give for such alliances is, that the discretion of the elder one shall curb the impetuosity of the younger.

At DEMERARY, the commissary court grant licences for marriage. Those who approach the altar of Hymen are generally people of colour, who, in conformity with the laws, are obliged to receive permission from this court, for which they pay the extravagant fee of one hundred and ten guilders. They are also obliged to have the intended marriage advertised in the Colonial Gazette. This form of marriage, though strictly binding under the colonial law, seldom satisfies without having recourse to a clergyman. An English Gentleman, who was on the point of marriage with a Dutch lady, attempted to break through this law, intending to be married according to the form of the Church of England; when the Vice-President, fearful of losing his fees, very charitably informed him, that, if he deviated in the least from the established custom, he would publish through the colony that they were living in a state of incontinency, and the consequent illegality of their marriage.

Mr. Bolingbroke, in his entertaining Voyage to Guyana, speaking of Demerary, says—"Family love, rare among us, is a natural virtue among them, of which all partake. Friendships may vie with those of fabulous antiquity; and, where such friendships are seen to grow, the families concerned congratulate themselves as upon an acquisition that promises to them a mutual strength, and to their nation the greatest honour and advantage.

"Agriculture, and the common domestic concerns, are the chief employment of the Indian wife; she plants yams, cassada, and maniac, in sufficient quantity to supply the family with bread, and with piworree, a kind of fermented liquor. The men are employed chiefly in hunting or fishing. No particular hour is allowed for meals, as the Indian eats when he is hungry.

"The females of Guyana endure little pain or after-illness from parturition. As soon as the labour is over, the mother and child are plunged in water, and the woman immediately goes about her usual occupations. Little care is taken of their offspring during infancy. The males, as soon as they are old enough, go hunting with their father, and the females learn the domestic duties of the mother. Indolence is a universally-prevailing feature in the Indian character; and, although the yam is so plentiful, and the earth so fruitful, that the greater part of their time is unoccupied, except by amusement, yet they are often in want of their usual sustenance. Their indolence is so great, that they spend a much greater part of their time in their hammocks that in active pleasures. Here an Indian will sit a long time picking the hairs out of his head, and then admiring himself in a looking-glass; then he will take a flute, and play upon it for some time; then he will eat, converse, and go to sleep. They are very expert swimmers, and are very fond of the exercise. Large companies of men and women bathe in the rivers several times a day, without the least regard to the indiscriminate mixture of the sexes; and sometimes they form large parties at each other's houses, when they divert themselves with stories, dancing, laughing, and drunkenness, which is frequently productive of serious disputes."

The native inhabitants of SURINAM, like the other tribes of Americans, conceive it a rite of hospitality to offer strangers their wives or daughters; and Mr. Stedman, in his interesting narrative, gives us the following entertaining account of the presentation of a young girl to him by her own mother.

"On the morning of the 22d, an elderly negro

women, with a black girl about fourteen, entering my apartment, it would be difficult to express my astonishment when she gravely presented me her daughter, to become what she was pleased to term my wife. I had so little gallantry, however, as to reject the offer with a loud laugh; but at the same time accompanied the refusal with a small but welcome present, with which they appeared perfectly satisfied, and departed with every possible demonstration of gratitude and respect. The girls here, who voluntarily enter into these connections, are sometimes Mulattoes, sometimes Indians, and often negroes. They all exult in the circumstance of living with a European, whom, in general, they serve with the utmost tenderness and fidelity, and they tacitly reprove these numerous fair ones who break through ties more sacred and more solemn. Young women of this description cannot, indeed, be married or connected in any other way, as most of them are born and trained up in a state of slavery; and so little is the practice condemned, that, while they continue faithful and constant to the partner by whom they are chosen, they are countenanced and encouraged by their nearest relatives and friends, who call this a lawful marriage; nay, even the clergy avail themselves of this custom without restraint. Many of the sable-coloured beauties will, however, follow their own penchant without any restraint whatever, refusing with contempt the golden bribes of some, while on others they bestow their favours for a dram, or a broken tobacco-pipe, or indeed for nothing. Dissipation and luxury appear to be congenial to the inhabitants of this climate, to which great numbers annually fall victims. Their fatal consequences are, indeed, too visible in the men, who have over-indulged themselves in sensual pleasures, and whose appearances are withered and enervated in the extreme; nor do the generality of Creole females exhibit an appearance more alluring; they are languid, their complexions are sallow, and the skin even of the young ladies frequently appears shrivelled. This, however, is not the case with all; and there are some who, preserving a glow of health in their lovely countenances, are entitled to contend for the prize of beauty with the fairest European. But, alas! the numbers of the last are so small, that the colonists, in their amours, prefer the Indian and Mulatto girls on account of their remarkable neatness and cleanliness, health and vivacity. From the excesses of the husbands, the Creole ladies generally appear in mourning weeds at a very early period, with the agreeable privilege of making another choice in hopes of a better partner, nor indeed are they ever long without another mate. Such is the superior longevity of females at Surinam, (owing, as before mentioned, to the excesses,) that widows may frequently be met with who have buried four husbands; but you will scarcely ever meet with a man who has survived two wives. The ladies do not, however, always bear with the most becoming patience the slights and insults they thus meet with in the expectation of a sudden relief, but mostly persecute their successful sable rivals with the most implacable hatred, and even on bare suspicion with the most unrelenting cruelty; while they chastise their partners, not only with an ineffable show of contempt, but also with giving, in public, the most unequivocal marks of preference towards those gentlemen who newly arrive from Europe, which occasions the trite proverb and observation in the colony, that the tropical ladies and the mosquitoes have an instinctive preference for the newly-arrived Europeans. This partiality is indeed so very extreme, and the proof of it so very numerous and apparent, that some command of temper is necessary to prevent that disgust which such a behaviour must naturally excite, particularly where the object is not very inviting; nay, it was once publicly reported at Paramaribo, that two of these tropical Amazons had fought a duel for one of our officers.

"In this colony, when a negro is purchased and attached to any estate, he acquires a right of settlement, and in youth and old age is maintained, clothed, and lodged. The old settled estates can boast of having reared negroes of three and four generations. Some negroes, not being able to accommodate themselves with wives on the estate where they were settled, were sent for to Stabroek, and taken to a sale-room, where a cargo of negroes was just landed, and there made choice of wives, which their masters paid for. Two chose pretty women, and the third an ordinary one. On asking him why he did not prefer a handsome wife, he replied, "No, massa, me no want wife for handsome, me want her for to do me good, and work for massa as well as me.' She was a stout young woman, and turned out much better than the other two."

When an Indian of Guyana marries, he is perfectly indifferent about the virginity of his wife, but after his marriage he expects fidelity to his bed; and so strong is the influence of opinion, that adultery is very uncommon, although it is not forbidden by any part of their religious tenets. Polygamy is universally allowed, but an Indian is never seen with two young wives; the only case in which he takes a second, is when the first has become old.

Pigafetta, in his Voyage round the World, remarks, that when he was at the Brazils, that the natives universally, for a hatchet or cutlas, offered them one or more of their daughters, but never their wives, nor indeed would the latter consent to have connection with any but their husbands; for, notwithstanding the freedom allowed to unmarried girls, when married, so great is their modesty, that they never submit to the embraces even of them to whom they are espoused but under the veil of night. They are subject to the most laborious toil, but are always accompanied by their husbands, who are extremely jealous. Their simplicity is easily demonstrated by their supposing that the boats, which either hung from the sides or followed the ship, were children of the vessel, and nourished from the hull,

At PORT DES FRANÇAIS, in the Brazils, Peyrouse says, the women are subjected to the greatest hardships, and perform the most laborious offices, suffering the utmost indignity from the men. Tattooing is not in general use among them; but all the women have their lower lip slit at the root of the gums, the whole width of the mouth; they wear a kind of small wooden bowl, which rests against the gums, to which the cut lip serves for a support, so that the lower part of the mouth juts out two or three inches; but none but married women are allowed to wear this mouth ornament, the young girls having only a needle in the lower lip. They may sometimes be prevailed upon to remove this bowl ornament, though not without much persuasion; they then testified the same embarrassment and made the same gestures that a female in Europe would upon the uncovering her bosom, or any other act esteemed immodest; the lower lip then fell upon the chin, and this second picture was no way more enchanting than the former.

Peyrouse informs us, that the women of BAY DE CASTRIES are not subject to any labour, which, like American Indian females, might change the elegance of their features, if nature had furnished them with this advantage. Their whole cares are limited to the cutting and sewing of their clothes, disposing of fish to be dried, and taking care of their children, to whom they give the breast till three or four years of age. The writer expresses his surprise at seeing one of this age, who, after having bent a small bow, shot an arrow with tolerable exactness, and, giving a dog several blows with a stick, threw himself on his mother's breast, and took the situation of a child five or six months old. The sex seemed to enjoy no considerable advantages among them. They never concluded any bargain with us without first consulting their wives; the pendant silver ear-rings, and copper trinkets, are peculiarly reserved for their wives and daughters. The dress of the women consists of a large nankeen robe, or a salmon skin, which they have the art of dressing so as to be extremely supple. This dress reaches as far as the ancle, and is sometimes bordered with a small fringe of copper ornaments, which makes a noise similar to that of bells.

In that part of South America called PARAGUAY, the women are allowed to propose matches as well as the men. When an Indian woman likes a man, she acquaints one of the missionaries with it, who immediately sends for the young man; if he do not like her, the priest endeavours to persuade her to overcome her passion; if, on the contrary, he is inclined to return her affection, the priest immediately marries and gives them his blessing.

The Indians of South America, when a couple are to be married, invite the relatives on both sides; the men bring along with them materials to build a hut for the young pair; the females present them with fish, fruit, bread, drink, &c.; the former chaunt couplets to the bridegroom, the latter to the bride; when it is dark the wife is presented to her spouse, which concludes the ceremony. Fathers possess such authority over their sons' inclination, that they must implicitly submit to give their hands where the father chooses. Instead of giving a portion to, he receives one from his new son-in-law.

In the Island of FORMOSA, and among some of the Peruvians, daughters are more regarded than sons, because she takes her husband home to her father's house, whereas sons, when married, leave their family for ever.

When a man fixes his affections upon a woman,

he serenades at the door where she lives, but is not allowed to enter; if the lady approve of him, she comes out, and they talk upon terms, and, if they come to agreement, the husband goes to live with his wife at her father's, instead of taking her to his own home.

In CHIRAGUA, when a girl arrives at a certain age, her female relations enclose her in a hammock, and suspend it from the roof of her cottage. Having remained in this hammock for one month, they let it down half way, and in another month the neighbouring women assemble, and with clubs strike furiously upon every thing within it. Having acted this farce for some time, they declare the serpent is killed which had stung the girl, and she is liberated from her confinement. All this signifies she is marriageable.

In the Brazils, and among some tribes of the Canadians, the sex, during the menstrual time, are shut up in a little hut by themselves; and, contrary to common custom in the Brazils, when a young virgin becomes marriageable, they burn or cut off her hair, make incisions from her shoulders to her waist, which is daubed with a corrosive powder. After a month, the incisions are repeated, and on the third she begins to appear abroad, when she is reckoned a delicious morsel for the arms of an ardent lover.

Among some other natives of South America, the *caciques*, or chiefs, are permitted to have several wives, while all the rest of the community are not allowed to have more than one. But, should they be dissatisfied with their wives, they can repudiate them, and make another choice. A father consents not to the marriage of his daughter until her lover has given unequivocal proofs of his address and courage. He betakes himself to the chase, kills as much game as he is able, brings it to the entrance of the cabin where she whom he is to espouse resides. By the species and the quantity of the game, the parents form a judgment of his talents and his merits.

NORTH AMERICA.

CANADA.——The Canadians are a swarthy people and low in stature, their dress consisting of a kind of jacket, and when the weather is cold, a blanket coat, which they fasten round them with a worsted sash. They are seldom seen without a pipe in their mouth, even from infancy; hence it is very usual in their houses to see the boys smoking. The women are extremely lively, good-natured, and obliging, but have not the least pretension to beauty. The Canadians have a very singular custom among them; at the commencement of the year the men go round the city and salute the ladies, who sit up for three days for that purpose, and, as the inhabitants are acquainted with each other, the lady is generally saluted by the greatest part of the men; the salutation is after the French fashion, upon the cheek, when, having saluted one, the lady presents the other. European ladies who are settled here, rather than appear singular, adopt this custom, only varying the salutation after the English fashion. The author of this remark, an English officer, observes, that he had a very great mortification in going to the house of an English merchant who had a beautiful wife; but, as the husband was there, and the salute must be given in his absence, a great disappointment ensued.

In Canada, courtship is not carried on with that coy reserve and seeming fancy which politeness has introduced among civilized nations.—When a man and woman meet, though they have not seen each other before, if he be captivated with her charms, he declares his passion in the plainest manner, and they answer *yes* or *no* without deliberation. In Formosa this simplicity would be considered as the greatest indelicacy.

MASSACHUSETS BAY.——The lower class of people here have a remarkable mode of courtship, which perhaps is borrowed from the native Americans. When a man falls in love with a woman, he first proposes his terms to the parents, without whose consent no marriage in the colony can take place. If they approve of him, he repairs to their house in the evening, in order to make his court to the young woman. At their usual hour the old people and the rest of the family go to bed, leaving the lovers together. Some time after the lovers go to bed also, and *bundle*, but without stripping themselves naked, to avoid scandal. If they are pleased with each other, the banns are published, and they are married without delay; if not, they part. Should, however, the woman prove with child, the man must marry her, or be excommunicated.

In PENNSYLVANIA, whenever two lovers meet with any very remarkable opposition from their friends, they go off on horseback, the lady riding before, and the lover behind. In this situation they repair to a magistrate, declaring that she has run away with her lover, and brought him there to be married, which is accordingly done. The same thing is a custom in the province of Old Mexico, where the bridegroom was carried off by his relations, that it might be thought he was forced into the state of wedlock, a state beset with thorns and cares.

In NEW ENGLAND frequently, when the moon is favourable, a number of young men and women set off on sleighs about seven in the evening, to join some other party eighteen or twenty miles off, where they carouse till day-light, and return to their avocation as if they had rested all night. This practice would be considered dangerous in England; but, after what has been said under the article of bundling, these nocturnal trips are considered innocent. Bundling has much declined along the sea-coast, but a similar practice is usual, called *tarrying*.

The ceremony of courtship and marriage among the MORAVIANS at Bethlehem, in Connecticut, is of that nature, that domestic endearments and felicity rest wholly upon chance, as no previous intercourse takes place between the sexes by which they may study each other's temper and disposition, the union of which is the foundation of happiness in the marriage state. When a young man feels an inclination to marry, he communicates his desire to the priest, (for he never sees his wife but once before the ceremony takes place, it being contrary to the principles of their religion to suppose it is from the passions of nature, but merely to uphold the society, that it may not sink into oblivion,) and asks of him a girl to make his wife, when the priest consults with the superintendant of the young women, and she produces the young woman who is next in rotation for marriage. The priest presents her to the young man, and leaves them together for an hour, when he returns. If they both consent, they are married the next day; if there is any objection, both their cases are very pitiable, but especially the woman's, as she is put at the end of the list, which amounts to near sixty or seventy; nor does the poor girl stand the least chance of a husband until she arrives again at the top, unless the man feels a second inclination for marriage, for he never can obtain any other woman than the one with whom he had the first interview; and this is probably the reason why we find so many old women among the single ones. Thus marriage and its inexpressible enjoyments are not the result of the passions, but a mere piece of mechanism, set to work by chance, and stopped alone by necessity.

When two parties meet and are united in marriage, a house is provided for them by the society, which is generally a very neat habitation with a pleasant garden. Their children, of either sex, at the age of six years are taken from them and placed in two seminaries, and hence arises the cause of the little affection they feel for their offspring. When either of the parties die—if the woman, the man returns to the apartment of the single men—if the man, the widow returns to a house that is built for this purpose.

At New Orleans the women, who in point of manners and character have a very marked superiority over the men, are divided into two ranks—the white and the brown. They have two separate ball-rooms in the city. At the white ball-room no lady of colour is admitted.

Those called the whites are principally brunettes, with deep black eyes, dark hair, and good teeth. Their persons are eminently lovely, and their movements indescribably graceful, far superior to any thing I ever witnessed in Europe. It would seem that a hot climate "calls to life each latent grace." With you the movements are rigid, and the muscles unrelaxed; whereas here the action is unrestrained, the muscles elastic, and the frame as supple as if destitute of bone. With you the form alone is fine and beautiful; but here the various charms of grace and symmetry are heightened by the most enchanting expressions of joy and elegance of motion. In the dance these fascinating endowments are peculiarly displayed.

The dress of the white ladies is very plain and simple; the robe white, fastened under the breast with a diamond pin, and the hair in the form of a coronet, connected by small bands of precious stones and pearls. The principal amusement of the young women of this place is to ride out after sun-set in small cabriolets, which they drive themselves with great ease and dexterity, a negro boy or girl, elegantly dressed, standing behind. In these excursions they are never attended by gentlemen, the loss of reputation being dreaded here more than the loss of every thing else. Their public amusements are balls and concerts, which are generally well attended; their private consist of music-parties at home and conversations around the door.

The ladies have much more reserve than French women; they are even distant in their manners, and it is not till they take a *fantasie* for a gentleman that they rise into friendship and descend into familiarity with him; after that period they kindle into love without much difficulty, and give that passion more dignity and embellishment than you conceive it susceptible of in Europe. A Spanish Americaine in love soars above her former excellence, and becomes a new object in the creation: so sensible is her lover of her attractions, that he too changes his nature, and, forgetting that the idol of his soul is human, looks up to her as a divinity, and offers at her shrine a suite of the most profound adorations. —Custom has made the church the theatre for the creation, discovery, and progress, of a first love. He who would gain the inestimable heart of a Spanish girl must attend her through a series of fervid devotions, gaze on her in reverential silence, or, at the most, in tender languishment express, "thy image steals between my God and me." If, in the course of an affair of the heart, conducted under the sanctuary and evidence of the church, the lover were to be guilty of any act of meanness and depravity, or sully his reputation in any possible way, his mistress would tear him from her heart.

The women of colour stand next to the white in society. They are very beautiful, of a light copper colour, and tall and elegant persons.—Their dress is widely different in general from that of the white ladies; their petticoats are ornamented at the bottom with gold lace, or fringe richly tasselled; their slippers are composed of gold embroidery, and their stockings interwoven with the same metal in so fanciful a manner, as to display the shape of the leg to the best advantage. A kind of jacket made of velvet, fitted tight to the shape, and laced or buttoned in front, with long points hanging down quite round the petticoat, and trimmed at the end with pearl tassels, is also worn; and on the shoulders of the jacket is fastened a cloak made of gauze, or some such light material, which hangs as a loose train to the ground, or is occasionally fastened to the side by a clasp of jewels. Their most general head-dress is either a handkerchief of gold gauze braided in with diamonds, or else chains of gold and pearls twisted in and out through a profusion of fine black hair, which produces a pleasing effect.—The bosom is covered with solataires, composed of every different kind of jewels. Notwithstanding the beauty and wealth of these women, they are not admitted, as I before remarked, to the white assemblies. They have therefore a ball-room of their own, which is well attended, and where as beautiful persons and as graceful dancing is witnessed as in any other assemblies of the sort whatever. A distinction subsists between ladies of colour of a very singular sort; those who are but one remove from the African cast are subordinate to those who are from two or three, or more, and are interdicted, by custom, from intermarrying with the whites; but they are allowed, by the same authority, to become mistresses of the whites without being dishonoured in the eyes of society; that is, they are esteemed honourable and virtuous while faithful to one man; but, if in their amours they at any time become indiscriminate, they lose the advantage of ranking among the virtuous, and are classed in the city books among prostitutes and slaves. This, or a native disposition to continence, has such a dominion over them, that they instances of their infidelity are very rare, though they are extremely numerous, and are mistresses to the married and unmarried, and nearly to all the strangers who resort to the town. For, though infidelity is punished among them, they are no sooner disengaged from one attachment than they are at liberty to form another. —The introduction of strangers to them is attended with some ceremony, and must be through the means of the mother, or the female adopted to supply her place. The inhabitants of the town never infringe their regulations or treat them abruptly, and strangers are instructed by their acquaintance how to proceed. The Levée at sun-set is the principal market for all this traffic *de cœur.* There all the beauties assemble, and there all those who need the kind companion joyfully repair: all walk up and down for a considerable time, or sit under orange-trees occasionally, with the objects of their separate choice. Such an expression of reserve, morals, and decency, reigns over the women of every sort, that a stranger passes and repasses before he can tell the one he admires the most *qu' elle est belle comme une ange*, and so forth. To an Englishman this timid, bashful, silent, demeanour opposes difficulties which require his utmost resolution to surmount, and he walks the Levée many a pensive evening before the sense of virtue is sufficiently consumed by the new passion of his breast to permit him to speak, or to offer terms to a parent, from which his soul shrinks, from the conviction of their being base and dishonourable. Some mothers now, on becoming acquainted with the English timidity, begin to alter their line of conduct, and suffer their daughters to remove their veil *en passant un Anglois*, or flirt their fan, or drop a handkerchief, which they receive with such gracious accents of gratitude, that a conversation may easily succeed.

The mothers always regulate the terms and make the bargain. The terms allowed the parents are generally fifty dollars a month; during which time the lover has the exclusive right to the house, where fruit, coffee, and refreshments, may at any time be had, or where he may entirely live with the utmost safety and tranquillity. Many do live in this manner, notwithstanding which, I have never heard a complaint against these interesting females. In proportion as they advance in age, they enter into service, &c. and are respected as much as when in their virgin state.

Negresses and female Mestizes next follow; the first are principally employed as servants, of which every family has a considerable number; the second perform all kinds of laborious work, such as washing, and retailing fruit through the city in the hottest weather; and, being considered as a cast too degraded to enter into the marriage state, they follow a legal kind of prostitution, without deeming it any disparagement to their virtue or their honour.

Among many of the American savages a married woman is looked upon as impure, infectious, and not fit to be in society, during child-bearing, suckling, &c. by which the greatest part of their lives they are excluded from social intercourse of every description. Indeed, the symbols they use at their marriage indicate the slavery and maltreatment they meet with, it being customary to present the bride at her wedding with a collar formed of a leather thong, a kettle, and a pile of wood; the first signifies she is to do all the domestic drudgery; the second, that she is to dress all the food; and the third, that she is to carry all the wood which the men hew. When the men hunt, it is part of their wives' business to seek the game which is killed, and bring it home; and, when the men have been fishing, the women unload the canoes with their child at their back, bring home the implements of fishing, &c. The husband's sole employment is hunting, fishing, and making canoes and weapons.

Among the NATCHEZ, the sovereign family suppose themselves descended from the sun;—therefore, if a female of that branch marry with a man who is inferior, she not only retains her dignity, but whenever she pleases can repudiate her husband, most generally behaving in the haughtiest style imaginable to them whom she has espoused. Not so with females who are not of the royal descent, their condition being the most abject possible, doing all the drudgery of life, while the husband lives in comparative idleness.

Mr. Ashe, describing the SHAWANESE, a tribe of Indians near the mouth of the Great Kenhaway River, after speaking of the women as handsome, describes a village supper, which was preceded by a dance of an hour. On descending to the river-side, he was agreeably pleased with the wild notes of some Indian boys playing a reed, which was intended to seduce the young women out of the village to meet their lovers in the woods, or wander with them by the stream. On the subject of love, it has been said they have no tenderness nor sensibility; but this mistake, Mr. Ashe observes, originates from their being forbid to waste their time in dalliance in the day-time; and were a young savage to tell his mistress before the sun had set that he loved her better than he did its light, she would treat him with disdain. Having returned to the village, he met a young Indian going a *calumeting*, which is a piece of gallantry here. As all property is in common, and the doors are open day and night, the lover, taking advantage of this, lights his calumet, enters the cabin of his mistress, and presents it to her; if she extinguish it, she admits him to her arms; if she suffer it to burn unnoticed, he returns disappointed, knowing that while there was light she will not consent to his wishes. Those nocturnal amours, however, often induce the girls to drink the juice of a certain herb, to prevent conception. This they do to avoid the disgrace of having a child, which is thought a thing so heinous as to deprive them for ever of respect, religion, and marriage rites.

Their marriages, says Mr. Ashe, are so simple, that they hardly deserve the name. "I witnessed no ceremony of the kind, but I understand from Adrario, a chief, that, when two young persons agree on the subject, they make known their intentions to their parents, who are not at liberty to refuse their consent, it being a Shawanese law, that the father and mother have no dominion over the person of a child. All the friends assemble at the cabin of the most ancient branch of the family, without respect to nearness of kindred, and there dance and enjoy a feast of great profusion and extent. After this festival all the friends of this party retire, except four of the oldest of each side, who require the couple to stand on a mat, and there attend a discourse on conjugal affection, and the charms of a chaste and honest mind. On which the lover breaks a small stick in pieces, and give the fragments to their friends, who keep them as evidence of the marriage, which cannot, while the stick can be put together, be denied. This ceremony is followed by inviting the nation to dance, sing, and amuse themselves till a late hour. The wedding over, the bride is conducted to her parent's home, where she is visited by her husband till she bears a child; and, if that event do not take place in the ordinary course of time, the parents assemble, collect the bits of broken sticks, see that they fit together, and then dissolve the marriage, by committing the testimony to the flames. Independent of this cause of dissolution, both men and women are permitted to separate at any time they think proper, giving eight days' notice, in order that the bits of sticks may be collected and consumed. It is worthy of remark, that these kind of separations are attended with no kind of dispute, quarrel, or contradiction whatever. The women are at liberty, as well as the men, to re-marry whom they may think proper, but in general they seldom enter into a second engagement till after the expiration of three or six months. On separation, the children are equally divided; if the number be odd, the wife is allowed one more than her husband.

"Notwithstanding this facility to change, I learn from Adario that advantage is seldom taken of it—in his nation not once in ten years; and an inviolate fidelity is maintained on both sides during marriage. As soon as a wife is announced in a state of pregnancy, the matrimonial rites are suspended, and continency preserved with a religious and mystical scrupularity till nine weeks after the accouchement. When a woman is on the eve of that event, she retires to a private cabin, *from which men are excluded*, and delivers herself without any assistance whatever. She remains there, attended by a few female relatives, while undergoing a purification, which lasts thirty days for a girl, and continues forty for a boy; after which she returns to the cabin of her husband. The poor child no sooner appears in the world than it is plunged into moderately warm water, then bandaged gently to a plank lined with cotton, and on which it is carried with great ease from place to place, or suspended from trees in the open air. The women always nurse their own children. That mother would be lapidated by them as a monster who would separate herself from her new-born child. When mothers lose their children before they are weaned, they have recourse to a very affecting and melancholy expedient; they search the woods for some young opposum, kangaroo, or other wild beast, and rear it with their milk with the utmost care and tenderness.

"The husband or wife dying, the widowhood continues six months. Mourning is not in use. In a single state, the Shawanese are susceptible of jealousy; in a married one, they are ignorant of that passion, the men conceiving that no person could be found suffieiently infamous to injure his neighbour's honour, and the women would suffer death sooner than inflict on their husbands so flagitious a wound. A married woman made this beautiful reply to a person who met her in the woods, and implored her to love and look upon him: "Oulamar, *who is for ever before my eyes*, hinders me from seeing you or any other person."

"The children always take the name of the mother. On asking Adario the reason, he replied, that, as the child received its substance from the mother, it was but reasonable it should transmit her name to posterity, and be a recompense for attentions and trouble.

"When a woman loses her husband, if he have left any brothers, it is expected that she should marry one of them after the customary period of widowhood; and, when a wife dies and leaves any sisters, it is understood that the husband should marry one.

"Among the Shawanese there are a few who observe celibacy: they are treated with great consideration; I could not learn why. Idiots are also treated with great respect: of the motive of this I am also ignorant. I have remarked that, when once a single woman bears a child, she can never after get married; and I should have added that, though many take drugs to prevent this misfortune, there are many who prefer pregnancy, which entitles them to lead without reproach a future life of freedom and dissipation. —This class of women are called *Tckoue ne Keoussa*, nymphs of the woods, because they are addicted to hunting, and associate with the men in all the perils and hardships of the chase. The parents never restrain them from this conduct: on the contrary, they appear to approve of it, saying that their daughters are mistresses of their own persons,—that they have a right to dispose of them, and to act as they think proper. The children are reckoned legitimate, and enjoy all the privileges of those born in wedlock, with this difference, that the chiefs and elders of council are not allowed to make them their heirs, nor are they suffered to intermarry into certain families, remarkable in the nation for military valour or political wisdom."

MISSISSIPPI.—In Major Pike's exploratory Travels through the Western Territories of North America, on the River Mississippi, near Clear River, he visited the lodge of one of the Indians of that tribe called *Fols Avoin*, who treated him very hospitably, and, after he had been regaled with elk soup, and had taken a walk round the other lodges contiguous, a good berth was provided for each of Mr. Pike's party of good soft bear skins nicely spread, and for the Major was placed a large feather pillow. The Major then proceeds:—

"I must not here omit an anecdote which serves to characterize more particularly the manners of the people. This, in the eyes of the contracted moralist, would deform my hospitable host into a monster of libertinism, but a liberal mind would consider it as arising from the generosity of the wild savage. In the course of the day, observing a ring on one of my fingers, he enquired if it was gold; he was told it was the gift of one with whom I should be happy to be at that time. He seemed to think seriously, and at night told my interpreter, "that perhaps his father (as they called me) felt much grieved for want of a woman; if so, he could furnish him with one." He answered, that with us each man had but one wife, and that I considered it strictly my duty to remain faithful to her. This he thought strange, and replied, "that he knew some Americans who at his nation had half a dozen during the winter." These, it was replied, were men without characters. The chief acquiesced, but said, "he liked better to have as many as he pleased."

Some of the American Indians, when they visited their mistress previous to the marriage, placed upon her foot the *otoia*, or shoe; that for a maiden was made of wool or cotton, but for a widow it was made of reeds.

Among some of the North American savages, adultery is punished in a female by her husband with the loss of hair, the nose, or perhaps life; such severity only proceeds from its having been practised without his permission, a temporary interchange of wives being very common, and the offer of their persons considered as a necessary part of hospitality due to strangers.

When a North American Indian marries, he immediately goes to live with the father and mother of his wife, who treat him nevertheless as a perfect stranger till after the birth of their first child; he then attaches himself more to them than his own parent, and the wife gives him no other denomination than that of the father of her child. Upon the death of his wife, it is looked upon as a duty incumbent on him to marry her sister, or he may have both at the same time if he chooses: some have three sisters, but they admit of no other relatives to their bed.

Observations on the Manners and Customs of the Female American Savages, by Du Luc, Heriot, and others.

'IT has been remarked that, among associations which have made but little advancement in the art of life, the condition of women is servile and degraded. The men alone may be said to be properly free, and the women, invested with the most laborious and domestic employments, are almost universally their slaves. In the women, notwithstanding, the property of the tribe, the distinction of blood, the order of generation, and the preservation of lineal descent, are by several of the northern tribes reputed to be inherent. In them is vested the foundation of all real authority. They give efficiency to the councils, are the arbiters of peace and war, and keepers of the public stock. The country, the fields, and their produce, belong to them alone. It is to their disposal the captive slaves are frequently committed. The rearing and educating infants to a certain age is their peculiar province. They are consulted in all marriages, and in their blood is founded the order of succession. The men, on the contrary, seem to form a distinct class among themselves; their children are strangers to them, and, when they die, every thing they possessed is destroyed or buried in the tomb with them. The family and its privileges remain with the women. If males only are left in a family, and should their number and that of the nearest male relatives be ever so great, the race becomes nominally extinct. Although by custom the leaders are chosen from among the men, and the affairs that concern the tribe are settled by a council of ancients, it would yet seem that they only represented the women, and assisted to discuss subjects that principally belonged to that sex.

Like the Lycians, the Iroquois and Hurons take their family names from the women, who alone are charged with preserving the race of their ancestors, by transmission to their children of the name borne by themselves. When a warrior dies, the appellation by which he was distinguished is buried in his grave, and is not renewed until the lapse of several years. The savages, in addressing each other, seldom make use of their adopted name. They apply even to strangers the titles of kindred; such as brother, sister, uncle, nephew, and cousin, and the relative proportions of age between themselves and the persons whom they accost. The practice of marrying a plurality of wives is more generally prevalent among the natives of the southern than those of the more northern parts of America.

It is common among the IROQUOINS when a women intends to marry, to leave to the principal matron, or some of his own relations, the selection of his future spouse. The choice having been fixed, and the consent of the female procured, a proposal is made to their relations, who hold a consultation upon the business; and, should it be agreeable, there is no delay in returning a positive answer. The marriage being resolved on, the friends of the bridegroom send to the cabin of the young woman a present, consisting of porcelain, pottery, blankets of skins, and other useful articles of furniture, which are intended as presents for the parents of the bride or her near ralations, as no dowry is expected with the bride. When the presents are accepted, the marriage ceremony is concluded. Men advanced in years frequently espouse young girls, as being more easily moulded to their own disposition.

Marriages are formed in such a manner, that the parties leave not their relatives and their cabin to have a separate dwelling and family, but each remain as before; and the children produced from the marriage belong to the mother, and are accounted solely her cabin or family. The property of the husband is kept apart from that of the wife, as the females inherit in preference to the males. The consideration of the children being entirely dependent on the mother, and forming the future hope of the nation, was the real cause among many of the tribes of the women having, in a political sense, acquired a degree of consequence superior to their husbands.

The married wife, however, is not only bound to give her husband food, and to cook his victuals when he sets out on an expedition, but likewise to assist his family when they cultivate their fields, and to provide fuel for the fires during a certain period. All the women of her own family, assisted by many others in the village, carry to the husband's cabin several bundles of wood; the wife, to recompence such as have aided her in this toil, distributes a portion of boiled maize to each; a formality which prevails only among the more stationary tribes, and is termed the *nuptial wood.* It is the office of the husband to make a mat, repair the cabin of his wife, or construct a new one.

The produce of his hunting expeditions, during the first year after his marriage, belong to his wife; afterwards he shares it equally with her, whether she stays in the village or accompanies him to the chase.

In the nation of the ALGONQUINS, where two wives are permitted to one husband, the one is considered of a rank superior to the other, and her children alone are accounted legitimate. They both inhabit the same cabin with the husband. The custom of marrying more than one wife, is no where to be met with among nations in a state of refinement; and the rules of virtue, as well as the precepts of the Christian religion, tend to its prohibition. Where polygamy does prevail, the women are less valued, and their mode of education is calculated to retain them in a state of mental darkness. In regular and limited governments, where property is secured to the possessors, legitimacy of descent becomes a matter of the highest importance. In proportion, therefore, as their conduct is regulated by propriety and virtue, women are held in estimation. The passion of love is of too delicate a nature to admit of divided affections, and its real influence can scarcely be felt in society where polygamy is tolerated. That refined impulse of tender and respectful attachment, the offspring of sentiment, is productive of the highest gratifications of civilized life, and its absence can by no means be compensated by the libertinism of barbarians. The Algonquins espouse without ceremony several sisters, and successively cohabit with the others; not visiting their wives in a state of pregnancy.

The ALPALCHITES of North America were permitted to marry in every degree of consanguinity next to that of brother and sister. Their children usually bore names which tended to commemorate the exploits of their fathers; though those of the enemies they had slain in battle, or of villages which they had burnt, were transferred to their sons. Among the inhabitants of New Mexico, polygamy is allowed, but those of Cibola take only one wife.

Although polygamy is permitted among the MOXES, yet it but seldom happens that a man will take more than one wife at a time, his natural indolence rendering him incapable of supporting two. Incontinence in the marriage state is considered a crime of the greatest enormity; and, if a woman is so forgetful of her duty as to be unfaithful to her husband, she is ever after reputed as infamous, and frequently punished with death. A total disregard of external forms seem to prevail in the celebration of marriages among the Moxes. The whole ceremony consists in the mutual consent of the relations of the parties, and in some presents on the part of the intended husband to the father or nearest connection of the bride. Reciprocal affection is by no means deemed an essential. After marriage, the husband follows his wife to whatever spot or situation she may choose to inhabit.

The CARAIBS, among whom a plurality of wives is permitted to an unlimited degree, have a right to espouse their cousins by their mother's side, who are considered as betrothed the moment they are born. The marriage does not, however, take place without the consent of the parents, and is considered an obligation of so trivial a nature, that it may at any time be dispensed with on the part of the woman.

The IROQUOIS, HURONS, and other nations among whom polygamy is not in use, espouse, after the death of their first wife, one of her sisters; they of the family of the deceased soliciting this new alliance, especially if they have been satisfied with the conduct of the husband. The same conduct is observed to a widow, and the brothers of her deceased husband. The state of marriage is not entered into by the man at an early period of life, his assistance in the chase being useful to the cabin or family in which he dwelt; it was, doubtless, with regret that he was permitted to form an alliance which would alineate his services and the fruits of his industry. The men, however, were generally so much attached to the family in which they were brought up, that they seldom discovered any impatience to break it by forming an early matrimonial alliance; and the habit of marrying at an advanced period of life may be attributed, perhaps, more to their own inclination than any interested motive in those they reside among. The passion of love, feeble, unless aided by imagination, is of a nature too refined to acquire a great degree of influence over the minds of savages. Their erratic mode of life,—their dependence for support on the precarious supplies which the chase affords, and their natural disposition to indolence, tend in a great measure to abate their ardour for the sex. This impulse, which bestows energy and comfort on mankind, they possess in a much fainter degree than the inhabitants of the eastern hemisphere. Many of the Indians are, notwithstanding, subject to jealousy, and often carry that passion to fatal extremes. The females, however, appear to be much more sensible to tender impressions.

Some of the Northern tribe conclude the marriage ceremony with a feast, in which the greatest profusion of viands is exhibited. The song, dance, and other amusements, vary the occupation of the day. At night, all the relatives of the bridegroom withdraw, excepting four of the eldest, who remain to accompany him. The bride is attended by a like number of females, one of whom presents her to her husband. The couple then, standing upon the centre of the mat, hold a rod, which is placed horizontally between them, whilst the eldest man present delivers a short harangue. In this attitude they alternately address each other, and sing and dance together, holding the rod, which is afterwards broken into as many pieces as there are persons present, to each of whom a piece is given. At the conclusion of the ceremony, the bride is led out by young women, who re-conduct her to the cabin of her father, where her husband occasionally visits her until her first child is born; on this event, her effects are carried to the cabin of her spouse, in which she afterwards continues to reside. Mutual separation takes place whenever it is the wish of the parties, who generally give a week's notice, assigning the reason of such separation. The small pieces of the rod which were distributed at the wedding are now collected and consumed by fire, in the presence of the husband and wife. These divorces are effected without dispute, quarrel, or contradiction. The women become equally at liberty with the men to re-marry when they are so disposed. The children, forming the wealth of those nations, are, at the period of separation, equally divided between the father and mother.

Although the privilege of changing is unrestricted, there are many savages that never have more than one wife.

Of some of the nations of South America, the men always sleep and live together in the same cabin; a practice which extends even to those that are married, who cannot enter the cabin of their wives but under the obscurity of night, their ancient customs not even permitting them to speak to the relations of the wife, taking every method to prevent their meeting with them, as though by their alliance they had become infectious, or they dreaded some injury from their resentments.

"It would be too long and too deficient in interest," says M. Du Lac, "to enter into a minute detail of the amours, &c. of each nation. I shall only relate the customs generally observed by the chiefs, who are scrupulously attentive to follow the customs of their ancestors. When a young man wishes to marry the daughter of a chief, he applies either to his father or some of his relations, who goes and entreats the father of the girl to consent. A definitive answer is never given until all her relations have been consulted. They examine how many brave men and expert hunters have been in his family; if there have not been enough of those, the match is immediately broken off; on the contrary, he gains the suffrages of her family. They are then entreated to supply the necessary expenses. Previous to this time he has never been allowed to enter the cabin of his intended, but, on the next day, he is carried in triumph to his wife, and her relations, after having made him eat and smoke with them, inform him he may come and live with his wife whenever he pleases. A few days after the marriage, the girl's brothers enter the hut, at an early hour, where the new-married couple have slept, and, drawing the husband from the bed, place him on a mat in the midst of the cabin. An old man then brings a vase filled with water, and, having washed the bridegroom from head to foot, paints him with red paint, and covers him with a skin. His brothers-in-law supply him with arms, &c. But he is not completely received into the family until a child is born unto him; then, and not till then, he is allowed to build himself a hut, and live where he pleases. Polygamy is tolerated among all the savages, without being attended with any inconvenience, as the women are taught to consider the men as superior beings, to whose pleasure they must be subservient. The women are generally kept in such a state of slavery, that they are not permitted to be present at their feasts. In each savage village there are some, who, through caprice or marriage, have left their own nations to dwell among strangers, by whom they are considered, especially in war time, as natives. Such are always employed to carry the first proposals of a peace."

At some of the villages visited by Du Lac the chiefs feasted him in turn, and according to their custom offered him their daughters, which he accepted of the principal chief, being afraid of displeasing him. The following are among the questions put to him by this people: "Are the people of your country slaves to their wives, like the whites with whom we trade?" Being fearful of losing his credit with them, he answered that they loved their wives without being their slaves, and abandoned them when they were deficient in their duty.

Du Lac, speaking of the American women in the maritime parts, says that the women in that part of the globe have fewer faults and more virtues than the men. If a young man is captivated with a female, he must provide her with every pleasure and amusement during their courtship, as the women, when married, expect no other amusement than attending to their affairs.

Mr. Hearne, in his journey from Hudson's Bay to the Northern Ocean, came to a tent of Indians near Thelewey River, where the chief, Matonabbee, purchased a wife, though he had six before, and most of them of the size of grenadiers. Indeed, strength here is more admired than beauty, as labour rather than love is looked for in marriage here.

Some of the women when young have personal charms, but work, bad fare, and ill-treatment, make them wrinkled at thirty. Just as Mr. Hearne's party was about to move, one of the Indian women was taken in labour, a circumstance which detained them two days. No sooner, however, was the poor woman delivered, than the tents were struck, and, with the child at her back, and a small bundle besides, she was forced to keep pace with the rest, often knee-deep in water. No wonder polygamy is allowed universally amongst Indians, when it is recollected that they are the greatest travellers on earth, and, having no beasts of burthen to carry the fuel, women supply their places.

The Northern Indian women are the mildest and most virtuous, while the Southern Indian females are remarkable for the dissoluteness of their manners, indulging in all the grossness of sensuality, and even in incestuous embraces. Reserved, however, as the Northern Indian females are, it is no unusual thing for their husbands to exchange beds for one night, a custom which brings no disgrace, but rather cements friendship; for, in case of the death of either of the men, the other feels bound to support the deceased's children, and is never known to swerve from the duty of a parent. Though the Northern Indians will have two or more sisters for wives at the same time, yet they observe a proper distance of consanguinity, but the Southern Indians make not the least reserve of that kind.

Mr. Hearne relates a story of an Indian female something similar to that of Alexander Selkirk, or Robinson Crusoe. A young woman of the Dog-Ribbed Indians was made prisoner by those of Athapusco in the summer of 1770; she escaped, and during seven moons supported herself in the woods, having lost every hope of finding her way out, and had not seen a human face. She was tracked by her snow-shoes, and, being a fine young woman, occasioned a strong contest among the party who should have her to wife, whence she was actually won and lost by ten men the same evening. Matonabbe, though he had no less than seven grown women and a young girl about twelve years of age, put in a claim, but he was shamed from this by one of his wives observing that he had women enough already. This irritated the chief so much, that he fell upon the poor creature, and bruised her so excessively, that, after lingering some time, she escaped from his tyranny and died.

Mr. Hearne, speaking generally of the Northern female Indians, says, though jealousy is a general passion among the men, marriages are contracted and dissolved with little ceremony. Young women have no choice of their own; they are matched to any man best able to maintain them, and, when children, are betrothed to men grown up, who, in case of their father's death, immediately provide for them. From eight years old to nine girls are strictly watched, and closely confined to domestic duties; but the parents set no bounds to the freedom of their conversation before their children. A divorce consists here in nothing but a good drubbing, and turning the woman out of doors.

In NEW ENGLAND the criminal law is as severe as that of the mother country. Divorces are authorized in cases of adultery or too near consanguinity. If a man and his wife have been parted seven years beyond sea, or if one or the other of them go upon a voyage of three years' duration, and there is reason to presume one or the other is dead, upon satisfactory evidence before a magistrate, a dissolution of the marriage takes place. Adultery was punished with death till the year 1784, but now it is changed to a public whipping, and branding with a red hot iron in the forehead.

The picture which M. Du Lac draws of the inhabitants of the United States is but little to their credit. The men are litigious, suspicious, and will not even trust their wives to go to market. "Every day," says the author, "convinces me that the women have fewer faults than the men. Balls, plays, promenades, and the toilet, entirely occupy their attention. If a young man becomes captivated with a lady, before he thinks of marrying her, he must provide her with every pleasure, and be accessary to all her whims. I have heard several American ladies answer to the most sincere declarations of affection, and to the most advantageous proposals of marriage, that they had not yet had time to know the world and its amusements, and that they would not retire without having enjoyed them." The young women are free when single, but slaves when married. They seldom then go out but to visit their relatives or to church, and are very much limited in their expences at home. Every lady suckles her own child. Female beauty here is of short duration, and there are few countries where the women have worse teeth than in the United States.

SOUTH SEA ISLANDS.

THERE does not appear to be any regular institution of marriage in these numerous and extensive islands; nevertheless, among that indifference which every where else prevails, they designate one female as their wife; but among the lower orders these ties are so easily loosened, that they can be scarcely said to bind the parties. Some account of them, however, may not be uninteresting, as their simplicity is very conspicuous.

Captain Wilson, who commanded the Duff on the Missionary voyage, says, " We found it very difficult to work up the bay, (Resolution Bay,) by reason of the heavy gusts of wind from the mountains. Though it was now dark, two females swam off, in hopes, no doubt, of a favourable reception; but, finding they could not be admitted, they kept swimming about the ship for near half an hour, calling out in a pitiful tone, Waheine! Waheine! that is, Women! or We are women! They then returned to the shore in the same manner as they came; our two pilots also followed them, but not till they had used all their arguments for the captain to allow them to sleep in the ship; and but for the sake of precedent their request would have been granted, as a reward for the implicit confidence they placed in us.

"Our first visitors from the shore came early; they were seven beautiful young women, swimming quite naked, except a few green leaves tied round their middle: they kept playing round the ship for three hours, calling Waheine! until several of the native men had got on board, one of whom, being the chief of the island, requested that his sister might be taken on board, which was complied with: she was of a fair complexion, inclining to a healthy yellow, with a tint of red in her cheeks, was rather stout, but possessing such symmetry of features, as did all her companions, that, as models for the statuary and painter, their equals can seldom be found. Our Otaheitean girl, who was tolerably fair, and had a comely person, was notwithstanding greatly eclipsed by these women, and I believe felt her inferiority in no small degree; however, she was superior in the amiableness of her manners, and possessed more of the softness and tender feelings of the sex: she was ashamed to see a woman upon the deck quite naked, and supplied her with a complete dress of new Otaheitean cloth, which set her off to great advantage, and encouraged those in the water, whose numbers were now greatly increased, to importune for admission; and out of pity to them, as we saw they would not return, we took them on board; but they were in a measure disappointed, for they could not all succeed so well as the first in getting clothed; nor did our mischievous goats even suffer them to keep their green leaves, but, as they turned to avoid them, they were attacked on each side alternately, and completely stripped naked.

"The natives crowded so much on board the following day, that with difficulty we carried on our work at the rigging; the females were more numerous, and all in the same natural state as before, which induced our people to bestow upon each a piece of Otaheitean cloth. It is proper to observe that these women dress decently on shore, but when they have to swim, as their cloth will not stand the water, they leave it behind, and wear a few leaves only.

"Two of the missionary gentlemen, Mr. Harris and Mr. Crook, having gone on shore to effect a settlement on the island for the instruction of the islanders, one of the chiefs, Tenae, it seems, wanted to treat them with an excursion to a beautiful valley, to which the latter readily agreed, but Mr. Harris would not consent. The chief, seeing this, and desirous of obliging him, not considering any favour too great, left him his wife, to be treated as if she were his own, till the chief came back again.—Mr. Harris told him that he did not want the woman; however, she looked up to him as her husband, and, finding herself treated with total neglect, became doubtful of his sex, and acquainted some of the other females with her suspicion, who accordingly came in the night, when he slept, and satisfied themselves concerning that point, but not in such a peaceable way but that they awoke him. Discovering so many strangers, he was greatly terrified; and, perceiving what they had been doing, was determined to leave a place where the people were so abandoned and given up to wickedness—a cause which should have excited a contrary resolution.

"Respecting the persons, dress, canoes, &c. of these people, we found them exactly as described in Cook's voyage, where he says "that, for symmetry of shape and regular features, they perhaps surpass all other nations."

"The women are rather of low stature, though well-proportioned, and their general colour inclining to brown. We observed that some, who on our first arrival were almost as fair as Europeans, by coming off to the ship and exposing themselves to the sun, became afterwards quite dark-coloured: but a few of these were punctured or tattowed. The chief's sister had some parallel lines on her arms, others slight punctures on the inside of their lips, and even upon their eyelids. They wear a long narrow piece of cloth wrapped two or three times round their waist, and the ends tucked up between their thighs: above this is a broad piece of cloth, nearly as large as a sheet, tied at the upper corners; they lay the knot over one shoulder, and the garment, hanging loose, reaches half-way down the leg.

"Of the infamous *arreoie* society at Otaheite the missionaries speak thus: "One of the arreoies, the tayo (or friend) of brother Henry, came to us with his wife big with child: they were taking their leave of us, in order, during their absence, to destroy the infant which should be born, according to the ordinances of that diabolical society. We thought this a proper opportunity to remonstrate with them against this horrid custom. The mother felt with tenderness, and appeared willing to spare the infant, but the brutal chief continued obstinately bent on his purpose, though he acknowledged it a cruel act, pleading the established custom, his loss of all privileges, and the total dissolution of the society, if this should become general. We offered to build them a house for the pregnant women, and take every child which should be born into our immediate care. Our brethren failed not to open to him the wrath of God against all ungodliness and unrighteousness of men. On this he walked off dejected, but not apparently determined to desist from the evil or danger of his ways. A few days afterwards he came, and promised, if the child were born alive, he would bring it to us, and on another visit afterwards with his wife renewed his promise, on forfeiture of our favour.

"The next day Pomarre and Iddeah, the king and queen, came at noon, and, going into the married brethren's apartments, found them conversing with the arreoies on the evil of destroying infants. Iddeah was particularly addressed on the subject, as she too was pregnant by a *toutou* who had cohabited with her, and was also of the arreoie society. Pomarre and Iddeah had for some time ceased to cohabit; he had taken another wife, and she one of her servants; but they lived in the same state of friendship, and with no loss of dignity. The brethren endeavoured to convince her of the dreadfulness of murder, in a mother especially. They then addressed Pomarre, and entreated his interference in suppressing such acts of inhumanity, and to give orders that no human sacrifices should be offered. He indeed appeared of a tractable disposition, and open to conviction, and promised he would exert himself to suppress such practices.

"We renewed our attempts with Iddeah, invited her to continue with us, and suffer our women to take care of her child; that her example would have the happiest effect upon the nation. She said the child was base born; had it been Pomarre's, it would have lived; but now they were arreoies—and marched off with her paramour, who sat by and heard with utter indifference.

Of the simplicity of some of the native women, it is said,—"One of our brethren this afternoon sitting in his berth writing, a young girl came in, and expressed her surprise that we behaved so different to them from what all our countrymen had done. He told her that such practices were wicked, and that if we did such things, our God would be angry." "Oh," said she, "but I will come to you in the night, and then none can see us."

In praise of the natives of the island of Tongataboo, the missionaries remark, "Their honesty to one another seems unimpeachable, though we have no reason to think the accounts of their dishonesty to strangers exaggerated.—The murder of children, and other horrid practices which prevail among the Otaheiteans, are unheard of here. Their children are much in-came in, and expressed her surprise that we behaved so different to them from what all our countrymen had done. He told her that such practices were wicked, and that if we did such things, our God would be angry. "Oh," said she, "but I will come to you in the night, and then none can see us."

In praise of the natives of the island of Tongataboo, the missionaries remark, "Their honesty to one another seems unimpeachable, though we have no reason to think the accounts of their dishonesty to strangers exaggerated. The murder of children, and other horrid practices, which prevail among the Otaheiteans, are unheard of here. Their children are *much* indulged, and old age honoured and revered. Female chastity is not much esteemed among the lower orders, it being a common practice with the chiefs, in our visits to them, to offer some of their females to sleep with us; the practices of our abandoned countrymen making them believe this a favour we could not well do without. Our first refusal seemed to excite surprise, but it has generally prevented a second temptation from the same person. Unchastity among females of rank, and especially after marriage, we have heard is punished with severity; however, we have not yet known an instance. Polygamy is in common practice among the chiefs, each of whom takes as many wives as he pleases; but they are entire strangers to domestic broils, which may, in a great degree, be owing to the absolute power each man has over his family, every woman being so much at her husband's disposal, as renders her liable to be discarded on the smallest displeasure.

"In TONGATABOO, their marriages are attended with very little ceremony. When a chief is attracted by a female, he informs his mother that he wishes to add her to the number of his wives; she immediately communicates this to the damsel's father; if it meet his approbation, she is clothed in a new garment, and with attendants, and as much yava-root, yams, baked hogs, &c., as he can afford, sent with her to her intended spouse, who, being apprised of her coming, seats himself in his house, and receives her in the same manner he would any other visitor, and with as little emotion; feasting on the provisions with a good draught of yava concludes the whole ceremony, and the bride is at liberty either to return to her father till again sent for, or remain in her husband's house.

"The natural colour of the inhabitants of Otaheite is olive, inclining to copper. Their eyes are black and sparkling; their teeth are white and even; their skin soft and delicate; their limbs finely turned; their hair jetty black, perfumed and ornamented with flowers; but we did not think their features beautiful, as, by continual pressure from infancy, which they call *touroome*, they widen the face with their hands, distend the mouth, and flatten the nose and forehead, which gives them a too masculine look: and they are in general large and wide over the shoulders. Their manners are affable and engaging; their step easy, firm, and graceful; their behaviour free and ungarded; always boundless in generosity to each other and to strangers. Their arms and hands are very delicately formed; and though they go barefoot, their feet are not coarse and spreading.

"As in all warm climates, the women in general here come earlier to puberty, and fade sooner than in colder and more northern countries; though in some the features continue little changed even to grey hairs; and what is remarkable, some are said to fade, and revive again, retaining their comeliness beyond those who have not experienced such a change. Many, indeed, who lead a dissolute life, receive their immediate punishment, and are old and haggard at thirty; whilst others, who have lived more decently, or, at least, have been less profligate, retain all the sprightliness and vigour of youth at fifty.

"As wives, in private life, they are affectionate and kind to their husbands, and uncommonly fond of their children: they nurse them with the utmost care, and are particularly attentive to keep the infant's limbs supple and straight. A cripple is hardly ever seen among them in early life. A rickety child is never known; and any thing resembling it would reflect the highest disgrace on the mother."

The missionaries resident at OTAHEITE give the following account of their marriage ceremonies. Early in the morning, the mother and uncles of the bride gave presents of cloth to their friends. In one of the houses a kind of altar was erected, covered with a piece of white cloth, upon which was placed some old clothes, that had enclosed the tomb of the bride's father. After the distribution of the cloth, the parties went to the family *morai*, or burying-place, where a large piece of white cloth was spread across the pavement, and the bride and bridegroom changed their dress; after which, the mother of the bride, with two or three female relations, took a sugar-cane, which, when broken into small pieces, they laid upon the leaves of a tree called *amai;* the mother, &c. then wounded themselves with shark's teeth, and caught the blood, which they thus caused to flow, upon the leaves where the sugar-cane was placed; they then presented the leaves to the bride and bridegroom, who were seated one on each side of the *morai*. The leaves, with the blood and sugar-cane upon them, were then offered to the supposed god of the family. In the instance from whence the above description is taken, the mother of the bride, who was advanced in years, appeared thoughtful, and produced the skulls of her deceased husband and elder brother, which, according to the custom of the country, she had preserved and anointe with cocoa-nut oil. The skulls were held befor the leaves, sugar-cane, and blood, at the tim of presentation to the parties. After these ceremonies, the cloth spread upon the *morai* was taken up and sent as a present to the chief. The clothes put on by the couple at the *morai* are considered as sacred, and not to be worn in common. There are also various forms that succeed marriage. If the woman be a virgin, the father and mother perform an *amooa*, or offering, of a hog or fowl, and a plantain tree to their son-in-law, before they may eat of his provisions; but not if she be a widow, or have been repudiated. The bride's relations make presents of cloth, hogs, &c. to the new-married pair.

In Otaheite, it is common when a woman does not agree with her husband, to cohabit with one of his servants, which is taken no notice of, nor is she looked upon as less his wife on that accounted; but the children of this commerce are most frequently put to death, for which, any more than adultery, there is not any punishment.

At Easter Island, Peyrouse was not able to ascertain whether the women were common property, or were attached to individuals; but they were very liberal in their offers of the women to strangers.

Polygamy is not practised at PORTLOCK HARBOUR, Prince William's Island, Montague Island, N.E. Coast of America. Captain Portlock, in his Voyage, observes, that no man had more than one woman, whom he seemed to consider as his wife, "to whom they pay very strict attention, and treat with a great deal of affection and kindness. You cannot affront them more than by attempting to make advances to their wives. They likewise are very fond of, and remarkably affectionate to their children. The women are the keepers of their treasures, or riches, which they generally have in a box or basket, and always take the lead in fashions, which they show by the *placing* of their ornaments, or fixing such a curiosity to be the favourite of the day. Men and women here, contrary to the custom in the South Sea Islands, eat together, which consists chiefly of fish of different kinds. The women here, were it not for the filth and nastiness which continually cover them, would be by no means disagreeable; their features in general are pleasing, and their carriage modest. They frequently gave us opportunity to observe their wish to please, particularly when the wooding party were on shore.

At these times they would place themselves in a line, and begin singing and making motions all the time the men were at work; and if their drollery happened to please the people and make them laugh, they all immediately joined in a loud burst of laughter. One time, not having the opportunity of sending the boat on shore at the usual time to fetch the wooding party on board, the women gave them an invitation to their habitations near the shore, and upon this occasion treated them with every thing their wretched habitations afforded, and behaved very kindly to them."

LOVE AND MARRIAGE.

AN ALLEGORY.

MANKIND were not, in their original state, divided into male and female, as at present; but each individual person was a compound of both sexes, and was, in himself, both husband and wife, melted down into one living creature. This union, no doubt, was very entire; and the parts well adjusted together, since there resulted a perfect harmony betwixt the male and female, although they were obliged to be inseparable companions. And so great was the harmony and happiness flowing from it, that these androgynes, or men-women, became insolent upon their prosperity, and rebelled against the gods. To punish them for this temerity, Jupiter could contrive no better expedient than divorcing the male from the female, and making two imperfect beings of the compound, which was before so perfect. Hence the origin of men and women as distinct creatures. Yet, notwithstanding this division, so lively is our remembrance of the happiness which was enjoyed in our primæval state, that we are never at rest in our present situation, but each of the halves is continually searching to find out the other half from which it was broken; and, when they meet, join again with the greatest fondness and sympathy. But it often happens that they mistake in this particular, and take for their half what no ways corresponds to them; by which mischance the parts will neither join nor agree, as is usual with fractures. In this case, the union is soon dissolved, and each part wishes to get loose again to hunt for its lost half, joining itself to every one it meets by way of trial, and enjoying no rest till its perfect sympathy with its partner shows that it has been successful in its endeavours.

When Jupiter had separated the male from the female, and had quelled their pride by so severe an operation, he could not but repent of the cruelty of his vengeance, and take compassion of poor mortals, who now could enjoy neither repose nor tranquillity. Such anxieties, such cravings arose, as to make them curse their creation, and think existence itself a punishment.

In vain had they recourse to other occupations and amusements; in vain did they seek after every pleasure of sense or refinement. Nothing could fill that void in their hearts, or supply the loss of their partners, so fatally separated. To remedy this disorder, and bestow some small comfort at least on the human race, in their forlorn situation, Jupiter sent down Love and Hymen to collect the broken halves of human kind, and piece them together in the best manner possible. These two deities found such a prompt disposition in human beings to resume their former state, that they proceeded in their work with wonderful success for some time, till at last, from some unlucky accidents, dissention arose between them. The chief counsellor and favourite of Hymen was Care, who was continually filling his patron's head with prospects of futurity; such as a settlement, family servants, &c.; so that little else was thought of in the matches they made. On the other hand, Love had Pleasure for his favourite, who was as pernicious a counsellor as the other, and would never allow Love to look beyond present momentary gratification, or satisfying the prevailing inclination. The two favourites became irreconcileable enemies, making it their chief business to undermine each other in all their undertakings. No sooner had Love fixed upon two halves, which he was cementing together, and forming into a close union, than Care insinuated himself, and bringing Hymen along with him, dissolved the union which Love had provided, and joins each half to some other which he had provided. To be revenged of this, Pleasure creeps upon a pair already joined by Hymen, and, calling Love to his assistance, they, underhanded, contrived to join each half, by secret links, to other halves wholly unknown to Hymen.

It was not long before this quarrel was felt in its pernicious consequences; and such complaints arose before the throne of Jupiter, that he was obliged to summon the offending parties to appear before him, in order to give an account of their proceedings. After hearing the pleadings on both sides, he ordered an immediate reconciliation between Love and Hymen, as the only expedient of giving happiness to mankind; and that he might be sure of this reconcilement being durable, he laid his strict injunctions on them never to join a couple without consulting and obtaining the consent of both their favourites,

Care and Pleasure. Where this order is strictly observed, the androgyne, or man-woman, is perfectly restored, and the human race enjoy the same happiness as originally.

REMARKS ON LOVE, MARRIAGE, CELIBACY, &c.

God has implanted in all his children a natural propensity to love and marriage.

When a man arrives at a certain age, he becomes sensible of a peculiar sympathy and tenderness to the other sex; the charms of beauty engage his attention, and call forth new and softer sensations than he yet has *felt*. The many amiable qualities exhibited by a fair outside, or by the mild allurements of female manners, or which the prejudiced spectator, without much reasoning, supposes these to include, with several other circumstances, both natural and accidental, point his attention to a particular object, and, of course, protract that propensity to a rambling regard, which is lost and useless among the undistinguished crowd, into a peculiar and permanent attachment to one woman, which ordinarily terminates in the most important, respectable, and delightful connexion. How very different is the state of human beings from that of the brute creation! The latter are clothed and generally armed by their structure, easily finding what is necessary to their subsistence, and soon attaining to their vigour and maturity, so that they need the attention of their parents but for a short time, and, therefore, nature has in general assigned to them short and transient amours; the connexion being natural, and merely for propagating and rearing their species, when that end is answered, the connexion dissolves of course. But the human race is of a more tender and defenceless constitution; their infancy and nonage continue longer; they advance slowly to strength and reason; they need constant attention, and a long series of cares and labours to train them up to decency, virtue, and the various arts of life. Nature has, therefore, provided them with the most affectionate and anxious tutors, to aid their weakness, to supply their wants, and accomplish them in those necessary arts, even their own parents, on whom she has devolved this mighty charge, rendered agreeable by the most alluring and powerful of all ties, *parental affection.* But, unless both concur in this delightful task, and continue their joint labours until they have reared up and planted out their young colony, it must become a prey to every rude invader, and the purpose of nature in the original union of the pair be defeated. Therefore, our structure, as well as condition, is an evident indication of the intention of Nature, that human beings are intended for a more lasting and intimate union. It appears likewise that the principal end of marriage is not only propagating and nursing our offspring, but to educate and form minds for the duties and destinations of life. Society must be supplied from this original nursery with its fairest ornaments and chiefest supporters. When our affections are placed on any of the sex, in whom beauty or agreeableness of person, and external gracefulness of manners, conspire to express and heighten the moral charms of a tender honest heart, a sweet, ingenuous, and modest temper, improved by good sense, it generally grows into a soft endearing attachment. When this attachment is improved by a growing acquaintance with the worth of its object, and is conducted by discretion, it becomes the source of many amiable duties, of a communication of passions and interests of the most refined decencies, of a thousand nameless, deep-felt joys of reciprocal tenderness and love, flowing from every word, look, and action. Hence friendship acts with double energy, and the natural conspire with the moral charms to strengthen and to secure the love of virtue. As the delicate nature of female honour and decorum, and the inexpressibls grace of a modest and becoming behaviour, are the surest, and indeed the only means of kindling, and ever after of keeping alive this tender and elegant frame, and of accomplishing the excellent ends designed by it, to attempt by fraud to violate the one, or, under pretence of passion, to sully and corrupt the other, and by so doing too often to expose the credulous and unguarded object, by a wanton and wicked cruelty, to the hatred of her own sex, and the scorn of the other, and to the lowest infamy of both, is a conduct not only unjustifiable, criminal, and base, but also inconsistent with that truly rational and refined enjoyment, the spirit and quintessence of which is derived from the bashful and sacred charms of virtue kept untainted, and, therefore, ever alluring to the lover's heart.

The mind is too apt to be dissipated in its views and acts of friendship and humanity, unless the former be directed to a particular object, and the latter employed in a particular province. When men once indulge in this dissipation, it is not easy to stop their career; they grow insensible to moral attractions, and, by obstructing or impairing the decent and regular exercise of the tender and generous feelings of the human heart, they, in time, become unqualified for, or averse to the forming a moral union of souls, which is the very cement of society, and the source of the purest domestic joys. Whereas, a rational undepraved love, and its fair companion, marriage, collects a man's views, guides his heart to its proper object, and, by confining his affection to that object, does really enlarge its influence and use. Besides, it is but too evident from the conduct of mankind, that the common ties of humanity are too feeble to engage and interest the passions of the generality of mankind in the affairs of society. The connection of neighbourhood, acquaintance, and general intercourse, are too wide a field for many, and those of a public or community are so for more, and in which they either care not, or know not, how to exert themselves. Therefore, Nature, ever wisely and benevolently directed, by implanting that strong sympathy which ever reigns between the sexes, and by urging them to form a particular moral connection, the spring of many domestic endearments, has pointed out to each the duties of their proper sphere, proportioned to their views, and adapted to each capacity. Besides, by interesting them deeply in the concerns of their own little circle, she has connected them more closely with society, which is composed of particular families, and bound them down to good behaviour in that community to which they belong. This moral connection is marriage, and the sphere of action, a family. Of the conjugal alliance the following are the natural laws. First, mutual fidelity to the marriage bed; disloyalty defeats the very ends of matrimony; dissolves the natural tie, the chief strength of which is in reciprocal affection, and, by making the offspring uncertain, diminishes the care and attention necessary in their education. Secondly, a conspiration of councils tending to the welfare of the common interest and education of their offspring. But, in order to observe these laws, it is necessary to cultivate, both prior to and during the marriage state, the strictest decency and chastity of manners, with a becoming respect of the respective parties to each other. Thirdly, the union must be inviolable, and for life, as the nature of friendship, and particularly this species of it, the training and instructing a family, the order of society, and of succession, which would be extremely perplexed without it, seem to require such regulations. To preserve this union, and render the harmony of the married state more complete, a mutual esteem and tenderness, a mutual deference and forbearance, a mutual authority and assistance, must be kept up. If either party attend to the duties of their station, there need be no disputes about power, nor *will there* be any. They have no opposite or separate interests, therefore there can be no opposition of conduct. From this detail, and the present state of society and religion, it appears that polygamy is an unnatural state; and should it be urged as likely to produce children, which is not the case, it may be answered, that it defeats the ends of rearing minds, which must certainly be superior to propagating bodies.

The Rev. Mr. Madan, some years ago, published a work that excited much attention from its novelty in a Protestant country, where bigamy is considered a heinous offence. This was a defence of Polygamy under the title of "Thelypthora," in which the arguments were drawn from scripture, and the uniform practice of the Jewish people, the patriarchs, &c. The ladies certainly disapproved of the tendency of such a work, and we have heard still less of any disposition here to transplant oriental customs on British ground. The morality of the times, as well as their pecuniary pressure, damp all experiments of this kind; nor is a British husband like an Asiatic one, who can divide his love without abridging his happiness.

"Whether," says an intelligent author, "polygamy is agreeable to the intention of nature is an old question. By that equality in the number of the sexes which almost every where prevails, it would appear that nature intended one woman for one man; and hence, that polygamy is contrary to her obvious intention. The same inference may be drawn from a quality of that passion by which Nature produces a union of the two sexes. Friendship may have several objects; Love only have one. It seems, therefore, that the union of the two sexes was intended only to be in pairs;

yet there are some reasons to believe that Nature intended more than one female for each male; women cease to bear children even in Europe before the fiftieth year, while men are capable of procreation to a much later period of life. Beauty seems to have been given to the female to invite the male to that union which is necessary for the existence of the species; the glow-worm lures the male to her embrace by a phosphorescent light. Beauty is the phosphorescent light, which was prepared to effect the union of the male and female of the human race; but this light is of short endurance; it goes out long before the male is incapable of feeling its influence. It seems to be a doubtful question, then, whether polygamy is not agreeable to the intention of nature."

All religions have permitted to men a plurality of wives in marriage; Christianity permitted but one, long before politicians had observed that the two sexes are born in equal numbers. All have boasted of genealogies, and, regarding with contempt most other nations, have permitted their votaries, when they had it in their power, to reduce them to a state of slavery. Ours alone has protected the religion of all men, and has called them back to one and the same destination, as to one and the same origin. The religion of the Indian promises pleasure in this world; that of the Jews, riches; that of the Turks, conquest; ours enjoins the practice of virtue, and promises the reward of it in heaven. Christianity alone knew that our unbounded passions were of divine original. It has not limited love in the heart of man to wife and children, but extends it to all mankind; it circumscribes not ambition to the sphere of party, to the glory of one nation, but has directed it to heaven and immortality; our religion intended that our passions should minister to our virtues.

It has long been a cause of regret, that the restriction of celibacy, laid on the fellows of colleges, has not been abolished in both of our universities. This was lately proposed in the Cambridge senate, but without success.

That a class of men, who are expected to set an example of virtue and irreproachable conduct should be excluded from a mode of life disagreeable to no other, is contrary to the dictates of nature, and hostile to the improvement of religion and morality. Unless it can be denied that clergymen are endued with passions similar to other men, no just argument can be alleged in favour of such an exception. We know there will be many adversaries to encounter, many obstacles to surmount, before this object can be carried into effect. We know that there are many, who, having passed as it were, their meridian, will discountenance it in *toto;* many will treat it with lukewarmness; yet, many there are who will be ready to espouse its cause. Among the objections started against this proposal, one of the principal seems to be, that the succession will become slower in every college: we grant it may be so, yet the vacancies occasioned by marriage are comparatively so very few, that no material difference will be felt. Others plead that the university will be rendered a scene of confusion, and that there will be an interruption to the discipline of it when filled with the families of the collegians. Others assert on the contrary, that it will be deserted by its professors. But both these disadvantages may be guarded against by proper regulations.

Let us, now, consider the evils that arise from this restriction; and it cannot be denied that it opens a door to perjury and immorality. A clergyman, respectable perhaps in eve: ther instance, when debarred from the happiness of an honourable connexion, is induced to enter into an improper one, which, if known, renders him an object of censure and disrespect. He gets preferment at a time of life when he cannot relinquish his old habits, and sits down to his living unenjoyed, when obtained, because he thinks it too late to form a nex connexion. Others there are, who, having at an early period engaged themselves to women of amiable manners and genteel education, are compelled to make up their minds to celibaey, till they get preferment from their college. Others again there are, who are tempted to infringe the laws of their respective societies, and clandestinely to commit an offence which may appear to them a venial one. Let the present members of our learned societies be objects of our attention, and some method may hereafter be derived to remove any detriment that may occur to successors. Let this proposal be allowed to pass the caput, that the fair opinion of the two universities may be canvassed, and let the heads exert themselves in support of a cause, which, both in a religious and moral point of view, seems so highly interesting and agreeable.

On the Laws respecting Marriage.

RESPECTING the view in which the law in this country considers marriage, it treats it as a civil contract; as to its tendency, it is regarded as all other contracts. By several statutes a penalty of one hundred pounds is inflicted for marrying any person without banns or licence; but by 26 GEO. III. cap. 33, if any person solemnize marriage without banns or licence from one duly qualified, or in any other place than a church or chapel where banns are usually published, unless by special licence from the Archbishop of Canterbury, he shall be guilty of felony, and be transported for fourteen years, and the marriage be void. Marriages, according to the legal forms of other countries, are valid in this. Parties marrying under twenty-one, must have the consent of their parents or guardians; and, if the mother be insane, or beyond sea, the Lord Chancellor will proceed upon relation in their stead. Marriages, within the Levitical rules of consanguinity, are not legal; but, if solemnized, are not void till after sentence of the episcopal court. To marry an heiress by force is a capital felony.

Bigamy, in law, respects either woman or man; and is when a second marriage takes place before the death of the first wife or husband. Formerly, this offence was punished with death, but it is now felony, with benefit of clergy.

In Bigamy, the first wife cannot be evidence against her lawful husband, but the second may, as the last marriage is not valid; and *vice versa* on the man's part. The Act allows five exception: First,—When either party has been abroad seven years; Secondly,—Where either party has not seen each other for seven years, (though in the kingdom,) and there is no knowledge that the other party is alive; Thirdly,—Where there is a divorce from *bed and board*; Fourthly,—Or wholly from the *marriage chain*; Fifthly,—Where the parties are under age.

Notwithstanding, the laws against Bigamy have received the sanction of the legislature and our religion, innumerable cases are always presenting themselves, in which these laws become cruelly oppressive. If a man or woman, after marriage, prove abandoned, drunken, insane, or prostituted, there is no redress; the reproachless party is compelled to drag on a life of disappointment and misery; and often flies to illicit amours or the bottle, for that artificial compensation which the law will not allow. In all cases of this kind, the law acts diametrically opposite to its intention: the unoffending are punished in mind, body, and estate, and the culprit enjoys the misery consequent to an indissoluble tie. In cases of adultery, the rich can obtain redress; but the expense of prosecuting a suit of divorce in the House of Peers, to annul a marriage, is an entire prohibition to a poor man's prospect of justice, and, as he dare not, without felony, venture to take a virtuous wife, and no prudent woman will marry the worthiest of men under such circumstances, the injured husband flies to unlawful embraces, and thus, in declining to offend against the laws of man, he violates those of God.

Divorces among the ancients were admitted on very slight grounds. The Jews obtained a separation without assigning any particular cause; but in the earlier ages of Rome, a divorce was unknown. Divorces are not admitted in Christian states unless upon sufficient ground. A Mahometan may put his wife away, and take her again to his bed, if she first lie with another man, called a *hullah*, who may retain her if he please. The Chinese grant divorces on the proof of various criminal or improper acts in the female. It seldom occured among the Orientals with the rich, because they were compelled by the marriage settlement to make provision for the wife. The Indians of America and Negroes divorce when they please; and the Siamese, in case of separation, divide the children, the women having the first choice. Adultery in all civilized and moral states has always met with severe punishment. In some with death, in others, with mutilation; and in most, with fine, punishment, or public disgrace, on both parties offending. The rude nations of ancient and modern times have also, more or less, marked their indignation at this depravity in the wife. Rapes also, both in a religious and civil point of view, have ever been the objects of severe punishment with legislators.

Viewing the condition of women throughout the globe, they have good reason to be satisfied with the treatment they receive in this country. Here a virtuous woman is always esteemed; and more respect is paid to character than to beauty. The sex are not drudges in laborious life, nor mere instruments of pleasure to the wealthy and the noble. A good wife is the companion and friend of her husband; and the law of England has so closely interwoven them, that it may well be defined to be one mind in two persons.

The happiness of life is involved in the act of marrying wisely, neither duped by passion nor yet without it. As Dr. Young says,

> Two kindest souls alone must meet,
> 'Tis friendship makes the bondage sweet,
> And joins their mutual loves;
> Bright Venus in her rolling throne
> Is drawn by gentlest birds alone,
> And Cupids yoke the doves.

Pope Innocent was the first who ordained the celebration of marriage in a church; before which it was totally a civil contract. And in the times of the grand rebellion, all marriages were performed by the justice of peace, and these marriages were declared valid. In Scotland, the parties being together as man and wife, or declaring themselves so before witnesses, makes a valid though informal marriage.

All legislatures ought to encourage the legal union of the sexes. The anxieties for the provision of a family are so many, that it acts with all the prudent as a restrictive barrier. Dr. Hally observes, were it not for the backwardness in marrying, there might be four times as many births as we find. By computation it appears there are 15,000 persons above sixteen, and under forty-five, of whom, at least 7000 are women capable of bearing. Yet, there are only 1238, or little more then a sixth part of these who breed yearly; whereas, were they all married, it is highly probable that four or six would bring forth a child every year, the political consequences of which are evident; hence those who have numerous families should be allowed certain privileges and immunities.

Great men have always been held in higher estimation as they have proved themselves good husbands and tender fathers. What can be more destructive to morality than to see the supreme head of any country setting the example of libertinism and incontinence? It is the manners of the higher ranks which give form and body to the lower; hence it is a gross dereliction of all law and justice to see the plebeian punished for the same crime which the prince may commit with impunity; and how gross is the absurdity, when the chief ruler swears at the altar to observe the laws of God, to promote true religion and virtue,—when he is designated in the formula of prayer—*most religious and gracious*, to see him setting chastity and temperance at defiance, and leading to perdition multitudes of subjects, whom, as the *head of the church*, he ought to labour to preserve! Let this principle also descend with equal force to inferior persons in authority, to masters of families, and to all whose example has influence in society. Felix trembled when St. Paul reasoned upon temperance, virtue, and a life to come, and could we have dissected that famous discourse, no doubt some parts of it would have contained cautions to the by-standers, that the best subjects are the best men, and that honour and the fear of God are inseparable. His allusions to the seducer of virgin innocence, of his neighbour's wife, to those who contaminate by example, must have been awful. Marriage, it is true, is not expedient to all, and the propriety of it much influenced by circumstances; but the Apostle in the most delicate and direct manner has *expressed* his sentiments on this head; though religiously an advocate for celibacy himself, he does not enjoin it where it may come in counteraction with propensities ordained by God, and sanctioned from the time of creation in the first pair. The Roman Church, taking up the practice and doctrine of St. Paul, has enjoined celibacy to the priesthood; but our church wisely has not made this essential to the true serving of God, for a clergyman is in his highest character when he serves the Deity by his piety, and his country by his paternal example.

It is a great misfortune that women generally pay too little attention to what they are worth. They uselessly employ themselves all their lives about beauty, to which indeed they can add nothing; and take no care to cultivate the mind, that most excellent field, which they suffer to lie fallow; their last sigh being often rather for the loss of beauty than of life. But let them know, that the beauty of the body merits our homage only when accompanied with the beauties of the mind. Nature seldom clothes with charms what is hurtful: the poisonous fruit is rarely pleasing to the sight: and let them ever remember, that *there is no monster in nature like a beautiful bad woman.*

Models of chastity and conjugal affection abound in ancient and modern days. Lucretia was a noble instance of the former, within the nature of this work. The history of Lucretia is so well known that it needs no detail; and t letters of Pliny and Cicero to their wives are fu of amiable and tender sentiments. A volume o letters of Cicero's are extant, and in one of them he thus addresses his wife Terentia, after he had been banished from his country by a faction that then prevailed at Rome.

"I must acknowledge that you have done

every thing for me with the utmost fortitude and the utmost affection; nor indeed is it more than I expected from you: though at the same time it is a great aggravation of my ill fortune, that the afflictions I suffer can be relieved only by those which you undergo for my sake. For honest Valerius has written me a letter which I could not read without weeping very bitterly; wherein he gives me an account of the public procession which you made for me at Rome. Alas! my dearest life, must then Terentia, the darling of my soul, whose favour and recommendations have been so often sought by others, must my Terentia droop under the weight of sorrow, appear in the habit of a mourner, pour out floods of tears, and all this for my sake? *for my sake*, who have undone my family, by consulting the safety of others. You present yourself before my eyes day and night. I see you labouring amidst innumerable difficulties: I am afraid lest you should sink under them; but I find in you all the qualifications that are necessary to support you. Be sure, therefore, to cherish your health, that you may compass the end of your hopes and your endeavours. Farewell, my Terentia, my heart's desire, farewell."

Through the interest and solicitations of Terentia, Cicero afterward returned to Rome, and re-possesed his honours and applause.

From every example, it appears incontestably evident that a happy marriage has in it all the pleasures of friendship, all the enjoyments of sense and reason, and, indeed, all the sweets of life: and to make it so, nothing more is required than discretion, virtue, and good-nature. But, for want of these, wedlock is now become the standing jest of fools, the curse of knaves, and the plague of most men. Where these are happily united, we may say with the poet,

> They know a passion still more deeply charming
> Than fever'd youth e'er felt; and that is love,
> By long experience mellow'd into friendship.

The Character of a good Husband.

THE good husband is one who, wedded not by interest but by choice, is constant as well from inclination as from principle: he treats his wife with delicacy as a woman, with tenderness as friend: he attributes her follies to her weakness, her imprudence to her inadvertency: he passes them over, therefore, with good-nature, and pardons them with indulgence: all his care and industry are employed for her welfare; all his strength and power are exerted for her support and protection; he is more anxious to preserve his own character and reputation, because her's is blended with it; lastly, the good husband is pious and religious, that he may animate her faith by his practice, and enforce the precepts of Christianity by his example: that, as they join to promote each other's happiness in this world, they may unite to ensure eternal joy and felicity in that which is to come.

The Character of a good Wife.

THE good wife is one who, ever mindful of the solemn contract which she has entered into, is strictly and conscientiously virtuous, constant, and faithful to her husband; chaste, pure, and unblemished, in every thought, word, and deed: she is humble and modest from reason and conviction, submissive from choice, and obedient from inclination: what she acquires by love and tenderness, she preserves by prudence and discretion: she makes it her business to serve, and her pleasure to oblige her husband: conscious that every thing that promotes his happiness must in the end contribute to her own: her tenderness relieves his cares, her affection softens his distress, her good humour and complacency lessen and subdue his afflictions. "She openeth her mouth," as Solomon says, "with wisdom, and in her tongue is the law of kindness. She looketh well to the way of her husband, and eateth not the bread of idleness: her children rise up and call her blessed: her husband also, and he praiseth her." As a good and pious Christian, she looks up with an eye of gratitude to the great Dispenser and Disposer of all things, to the husband of the widow and father of the fatherless, intreating his divine favour and assistance in this and every other moral and religious duty; well satisfied, that, if she duly and punctually discharge her several offices in this life, she shall be blessed and rewarded for it in another. "Favour is deceitful, and beauty in vain; but a woman that feareth the Lord, she shall be praised."

Sentiments of Mr. Penn on Marriage.

NEVER marry but for love, but see that thou love what is lovely.

If Love be not thy chiefest motive, thou wilt soon grow weary of the married state, and stray from thy promise to search out thy pleasures in forbidden places.

Let not enjoyment lessen, but rather augment affection; it being the basest of passions to slight what we sighed to possess.

It is the difference betwixt love and lust, that love is fixed; that volatile love grows, but lust wastes, by enjoyment. And the reason is this,—that one springs from a union of souls, and the other from a mere union of sense. They have diverse originals, and so are of different families: One is inward and deep, the other superficial; one is permanent, the other transient.

They that marry for money cannot have the true satisfaction of marriage, the more essential requisite being wanting.

Men are frequently more careful in breeding their horses and dogs than their children. The former must be of the best sort for shape, strength, and courage; but as for the latter, their own posterity, *money* shall answer all *things*. With such, it makes the crooked straight, sets squint-eyes right, cures madness, covers folly, changes ill conditions, mends the skin, gives a sweet breath, repairs honours, makes young, and works wonders.

Oh! how sordid is Man grown! Man, the noblest creature in the world! As a God on the earth, and the image of him that made it, thus to mistake earth for heaven, and worship gold for God.

Maxims in the choice of a Wife—conduct towards her, &c.

TAKE unto thyself a wife, and obey the ordinance of God; take unto thyself a wife, and become a faithful member of society. But examine with care, and fix not suddenly. On thy present choice depends the future happiness of thee and thy posterity. If much of her time is destroyed in dress and ornaments; if she be enamoured of her own beauty, and delighted too much with her own praise; if she laugheth much, and talketh very loud; if her foot abideth not in her father's house, and her eyes, with boldness, rove much on the faces of men; though her beauty were as the sun in the firmament of heaven, turn thy face from her charms; turn thy feet from her paths, and suffer not thy soul to be ensnared by the allurements of thy imagination. But, when thou findest sensibility of heart joined with softness of manners, an accomplished mind with a form agreeable to thy fancy, take her home to thy house, she is worthy to be thy friend, thy companion for life, the wife of thy bosom. Oh! cherish her as a blessing sent thee from heaven; let the kindness of thy behaviour endear thee to her heart.

She is the mistress of thy house, treat her therefore with respect, that thy servants and all around thee may also treat her with a due regard.

Oppose not her inclination without cause; she is the partner of thy cares, make her also the companion of thy pleasures.

Reprove her faults with gentleness, exact not her obedience with rigour.

Trust thy secrets in her breast; her counsels are sincere, thou shalt not be deceived.

Be faithful to her bed; she is the mother of thy children.

When pain and sickness assault her, let thy tenderness sooth her affliction. A look from thee of pity and love shall alleviate her grief, or mitigate her pain; and be of *more avail than* ten physicians,

Consider the delicacy of her sex, the tenderness of her frame, and be not severe to her weakness, but remember thine own imperfections.

FINIS.